UNCERTAIN TIMES
"THE GREAT CHANGE"

A guide for the unpredictable Change

Juan Ferrer

UNCERTAIN TIMES. THE GREAT CHANGE

All rights reserved. Any reproduction of this work in whole or in part, or its inclusion on any information system, or transmission in any form or by any medium (electronic, mechanical, photocopy, recording or others) without the prior express written permission of the copyright holder is strictly prohibited. Copyright infringement may constitute a crime against intellectual property.

Edition: Independently published

© Juan Ferrer, 2020

INDEX

INTRODUCTION 9

CHAPTER ONE
GLOBALIZATION – DEGLOBALIZATION 13
    The butterfly effect 18
    Dependence 21
    Rules and values 24
    Winners and losers 26
    Deglobalization 33
    Global governance 35

CHAPTER TWO
WORK IN THE FUTURE 39
    Technology, robots and digitization 42
    The new professions 48
    Employee or freelancer 50
    Talent 53
    Opportunities 54
    Telework 56
    Reinvent of recycle 58

CHAPTER THREE
THE NEW ECONOMY 61
    Digital economy 63
    Circular economy 65
    Collaborative economy 67
    Sustainable economy 69
    Real economy 70
    Financial economy 72
    The debt 74

The cartels	77
Production and consumption	80
The crises	83
The inequalities	85
Tax havens	89

CHAPTER FOUR
THE OTHER POLITICS	93
Bipartisanship - multi-partisanship	94
Leaders	97
Good politics	99
Bad politics	101
Populism	103
Lefts - rights	106
The weight of the state	110

CHAPTER FIVE
DEMOGRAPHY	113
The juniors	118
The seniors	121
Trends	125

CHAPTER SIX
THE CRISES	129
Brief history	131
The causes	135
The consequences	136
The exit	138

CONCLUSION
"REINVENTING YOURSELF"	141

*Dedicated to my parents,
two good people
and my two children
Isabel and Pablo.*

INTRODUCTION

*"Life is like a rudderless boat in
the middle of a storm."
(Pio Baroja, tetralogy of the sea)*

    This book is about The Change in general that has been coming about in society since the mid 20th century and the beginning of the 21st century, currently and in the near future, which is influencing all levels of social life and at a personal level; forcing us to constantly reassess our ideas, our habits, our jobs, our social relationships and our customs. In short, it forces us to reinvent ourselves each day if we do not want to be relegated to the margin of society and from ourselves.

Until the middle of the 20th century, practically everything was largely fixed and stable; institutions, beliefs, religion, and above all work and professions; for centuries the baker's son would become a baker, the carpenter's son would become a carpenter, and the son of the blacksmith would become a blacksmith or the son of a doctor would become a doctor. Since the end of the nineteen sixties, so many changes have come about and at such a rapid pace that both society as a whole and individuals have had trouble sifting through them and begin adapting gradually to a permanent and accelerated change, provoking radical and disruptive changes in both society and individuals. This carries with it a thought transformation and more important still, in the attitudes and customs of the people and in their behavior.

We've all seen or heard either on television or on our mobile phones the daily forecast of what the weather will be like in the coming days or even weeks with a relatively high degree of certainty due to the development of predictive technology based on mathematical models and applied in an almost routine manner. Essentially, we do this to satisfy the human need to know what the future has in store for us, on one hand, to calm our vital anguish, on the other hand, to be better prepared for how these future changes may affect our businesses or enterprises, our farmers, our travel plans or even our habits, in essence our lives; deep down we do it to satisfy that ancestral human need for security, in the end, it is no more than the unconscious survival instinct.

That said, since the dawn of man, he has always had to deal with the external and fortuitous elements that nature has continuously presented him with in diverse forms, from a storm, an earthquake, a war, a plague, a pandemic, a volcanic eruption or the attack of a wild animal; or even climate change across the different epochs of history. Human beings have been capable of dealing with and overcoming all of these randomly occurring changes and events on multiple occasions since their origins on Earth. On one hand, this demonstrates the enormous capacity for resistance (resilience) which humans possess, on the other hand, it reaffirms that innate need for security which men have a tendency for, precisely to placate in great measure, the generally adverse consequences of these events which would put in peril their own survival.

Events of all sorts will take place throughout our lives, some expected, others unexpected which will influence and even change the course of our lives in an important way. Within the expected events there may be such things as planning a vacation, completing an education, finding a job, etcetera... and these types of events, although they influence our lives, rarely do so in a decisive way, for having been expected and planned, we know with a fair amount of certainty what their consequences will be. Notwithstanding, once in a while and throughout life, unexpected and unforeseen events take place which influence and change the course of our lives in radical ways; it happens when a war is unleashed whose end result is always uncertain; or a natural disaster, a great recession, a grave illness or an accidental death... or as the writer Nassim Taleb said, when "A black swan" appears, referring to the last great economic crisis that happened in 2008. Life does not always move forward, sometimes it moves backward.

It is for the latter type of events that we should be better prepared, if not physically, as they are unforeseen, then mentally and with the right attitude, so that when they do happen we are not caught unprepared for the grave consequences that follow, as we've seen with the Covid-19 crisis all over the world.

In spite of this, why were there countries that overcame the pandemic better than others?... there are three key words in corporate management, they are: Anticipation, Planning and Management. One example of these have been countries such as South Korea, Taiwan, New Zealand and Australia. This is the most recent example that we have, but throughout the distinct chapters of the book, we will attempt to explain within the possible realm why these exceptional events come to be, given that there are almost always "warnings" or "reasonable premonitory indicators", such as those employed by the justice system to prove a fact, and what consequences they have on our lives.

The book has various chapters about Change and the changes that are coming about through Globalization, at work, in the economy, technological advancements, digitalization, robotics, telework, the Youth and their future, demographic changes and senior citizens, new platforms for social relations, new professions, new ways for political engagement… in short, the key word is Change and how is forces us to rethink and reassess our lives facing the future. As I've said, this implies a change in mentality and attitude in people; we stand before a new paradigm: "Nothing is stable and everything Changes", and the objective of this book is to help understand and see more clearly what is happening in society with the goal that it may help many people change their mentality and their way of seeing things and to shed some light on future threats that these changes represent and how they may affect their lives in these moments and in the future; most of all to those who believe that things do not change, that everything remains the same, that the greatest security and stability comes from being a civil servant, or keeping a job, and also those who think that their current status will last forever. This book is not for entertainment or even education, this is a book of information and knowledge; this book is about "Changes" and "Warnings", about "Indicators" and "Threats", about "Attitudes", "Planning" and "Management in uncertainty". The only two things that are certain in life are: Death and CHANGE; and it is best to be prepared for it.

Throughout the following chapters, we will attempt to explain a good part of what is happening and help and advise, within the realm of possibility, how to be better prepared or emerge in a better state from those circumstances. The changes discussed in the book were already in motion long before the pandemic arrived. All it has done is accelerate them, like what has happened with teleworking and e-commerce.

CHAPTER ONE

GLOBALIZATION - DEGLOBALIZATION

The phenomenon of Globalization is nothing new and has been among us for more than five thousand years. When the Assyrians exported their wheat surplus and textiles from the banks of the Tigris and Euphrates and exchanged them for the copper extracted from the mountains of Sinai there was already a form of globalization in action for thousands of years. When Marco Polo traveled to China in search of prized silk to bring back to the European Courts where it was most appreciated, thereby giving new impetus to the "Silk Road" on which Rome traded with China since the first century, it was also a form of globalization in which the point of origin was the exchange of mercantile and its by-product, a social and cultural exchange which at its core was the origin of what we now call International Commerce and more recently: Globalization. As Adam Smith said, man has a natural "propensity" to "trade, barter and exchange some things for others". In this day and age, Globalization is an entirely consolidated act and accepted by the entire world as a permanent and constant process of the free exchange of goods, capital, services and people between all the countries in the world. This process has been propelled and accelerated for more than three thousand years, but it is above all, since the middle of the last century with the fall of the walls in many countries, the reduction of international transport costs, and with the drastic drop and in many cases the suppression of a majority of the tax barriers in countries, whose end goal throughout history has been none other than to protect their borders and Gross Domestic Products (GDP), producing a vertiginous acceleration of time and space... the walls have fallen and societies have become more open, propelled by the internet phenomenon and the exponential growth of connectivity around the world.

Globalization has actually reached another dimension, more ample and rich than the mere exchange of merchandise as it was originally, and has gone on to be a global phenomenon that influences daily and on occasion in important ways the lives of the majority of people in all the world. Today, Globalization is characterized firstly by the integration of the majority of countries in one single physical and virtual market via the internet and secondly, by the almost instant connectivity which accelerates the interactions between people and countries from different regions of the world.

Just a few hundred years ago, taking merchandise from one country to another may have meant months or years with the consequential risks and the high cost of transportation this would entail for delivery of that merchandise, when on many occasions they were lost or stolen along the way. Nowadays, however, the same merchandise may be transported from one country to another thousands of kilometers away on the same day and sometimes in hours with complete security.

However, the most relevant thing of all that is happening and which we call Globalization is not only the gains produced by the increased speed, productivity and efficiencies generated by the new globalizing phenomenon, but rather the increase of benefits and wellbeing that this new form of production and trade has generated in people, ideas, methods, and the culture of the majority of people and countries.

Of course Globalization, like almost everything in life, also has another less amenable and positive face, and this process has also punished many people and countries in an unjust manner, as we see it, you only have to look at the great protests that come about in certain areas of the world that are led by new social movements when the powers in charge of promoting Globalization come together periodically, such as the IMF, the World Bank, or the World Trade Organization.

In recent years, we've all known or heard talk about the case of some corporations that have outsourced all or part of their production operations to another country with lower costs, primarily to Southeast Asia or Africa. The immediate consequences of this decision may be seen reflected in the following example: a worker at a European company is laid off as his job will now be done by a worker in Vietnam; the Vietnamese worker may now buy a small apartment and go on vacation once a year, thereby becoming a part of his country's middle class; on the contrary, the European worker who lost their job begins to have serious financial difficulties, this situation leads to unpaid bills and finally, the bank foreclosing on their home.

Meanwhile, for the head of the company employing the Vietnamese worker things are going very well, with more orders coming in regularly and increasing sales each year; by in the end, the businessman decides to buy a home in Europe as an investment and so that his children may, eventually, go there to study. Coincidentally, he buys the foreclosed property of the displaced worker whose job was outsourced to Asia which is now up for sale. It makes no difference to the bank as it has been able to sell the property to a new client, but it has created a redistribution of wealth for the buyer's country as a result of so called Globalization.

Hence, the obvious question we may ask ourselves is: Globalization has been good or bad and for whom? In this concrete example, it is evident that it has been bad for the European worker and good for the Vietnamese worker and his boss. However, if we look at it globally, perhaps, it may not have been so bad, since upon seeing their situation worsen, the European worker signed up for a retraining course in a new technology currently in high demand, within a few months, they were able to obtain a new and better paying job than their previous one, since they now have added value and after some time they were able to buy another apartment and rejoin the middle class from which they had been let down when they lost their previous employment.

I know that in many cases things don't happen in such a positive way and that many workers are left hanging off of the change train, but unfortunately as the economist Joseph A. Shumpeter would say, one of the mechanisms of advancing capitalism consists of the "Creative destruction", that is to say, allowing the old to die to make way for the new and what brings more value to the economy.

In the end, these processes, while painful for millions of people all over the world, are not exclusive of the economic mechanisms or uniquely of the logic of capitalism, if we cautiously observe, these situations happen in most areas of life, in nature, in politics, in the different systems, in people and in societies. Many times we must let the old die to make way for the new, in order to create new methods of production, distribution and social relations that in the end will benefit a greater number of people and the world in general.

However, without wanting to recreate an excessively idyllic view, the redistribution of wealth, jobs and capital assets will greatly benefit the more advanced countries by allowing them to focus on the production of higher value added assets and services, as they have the most qualified workforce and most advanced technological systems at their disposal. Likewise, for developing countries, this process represents an opportunity to emerge from primitive subsistence agriculture or livestock systems, into a second arena of an industrial economy and mass production and at the same time, acquire knowledge and technology for the establishment of many companies in their country, that were previously nonexistent, and will certainly benefit the majority of the population of those countries.

Although it's true that in everything that has been written about the phenomenon of Globalization we may find enthusiastic promoters of this current, there are also multitudes of people and organizations that are not as optimistic, but rather openly attack and despise the supposed benefits produced by Globalization. It is not the purpose of this book to engage in a theoretic and real discussion about the consequences of the Globalization process, instead we will limit ourselves to giving our opinion about what is occurring, the changes that are coming and their consequences, like a good social observer.

Globalization may be the most powerful process and that which has given the most growth and wellbeing to millions of people and numerous countries in the last few decades, but it can also be a destructive force which has caused much pain and prejudice to other countries according to Ian Goldin, professor at the Martin School, Oxford University. Globalization has brought innumerable benefits to society through the exchange of technology, work, medicine with the vaccines, nutrition, ideas, and merchandise; but it has also generated many prejudices and much harm in different countries such as pandemics, terrorism, great crises, climate change and inequalities in some parts of the world. Globalization has been very beneficial for one part of the population, those who had greater resources, a higher education and better information.

Nevertheless, the same has not occurred and it has been quite pernicious and negative for another part of the population that did not have access to those same resources, the same education, nor were they as well informed, that is to say, for many countries on a development track.

THE BUTTERFLY EFFECT

Edward Lorenz was a meteorologist from the Massachusetts Institute of Technology (MIT), who tried to explain why it is so difficult to make meteorological predictions giving way to what is known today as the Chaos Theory. In an article published in 1972 and titled Forecasting: Can the flapping of a butterfly's wings in Brazil cause a tornado in Texas? He set the bases of a series of mathematical models which are known today as The Butterfly Effect and which have had great repercussions in various branches of science; in fact, by way of this theory we may study phenomena such as population growth or pandemics, the migration of schools of fish and migratory birds or even cerebral function and weather forecasting.

No one is forgetting that the recent pandemic produced by Covid-19 and whose origin is situated in China has been one of the most devastating events humanity has recently suffered, which has affected nearly every country in the world and whose nefarious consequences will linger among us for a good period of time. Likewise, we all remember the fall of Lehman Brothers Investment Bank in 2008, the origin of a major financial crisis and the terrible consequences, especially economic ones, that it brought about in the world financial system affecting millions of people and corporations.

We are not going to delve into the details and into the circumstances that have accompanied these phenomena known by all, as there is sufficient information and bibliography about these events, and in the end, is not this book's objective. However, we have wanted to mention it for its relevance and for the grave and important consequences that it will leave in our world, and which serves as an example of the scientific basis we have just mentioned; since events or developments of this kind come to corroborate how the events occurring in one part of the world could have dramatic and unforeseeable repercussions in other regions due to the great independence and integration of all countries in the actual world.

More recently, in a stupendous article published in the daily newspaper El Pais about these questions and signed by the journalist Jorge Benitez, reference is made to a metaphor ideated by the political analyst Michelle Wucker who refers to those threats which we know exist, but which we cannot stop and which she calls "the gray rhinoceros" referring to any relevant event, like a massive cyber attack, a social revolt, or even a nuclear accident. The response of the majority of the political class has been "no one could have prevented what happened" …they lie, she says, and on that we agree, when we pointed out at the beginning of the book that ahead of these types of phenomena there are almost always "warnings", "indicators" or even predictions as has effectively occurred in this case and which is paradigmatic as it was somehow forecast, at least as a theoretical exercise, by Bill Gates in that premonitory TED Talk conference in 2015 which many of us have seen on channels like YouTube and other mediums.

Many other cases exist, although perhaps not as grave, such as the eruption of the Bardarbunga Volcano in Iceland in 2014 which caused the near complete grounding of thousands of flights in that region over a period of several weeks with the grave consequences that event produced in the economy and worse still in the environment.

At the start of this century, in the years 2000 and 2001 a series of conjoined and consecutive episodes of severe drought and flooding happened in dozens of Asian countries, which caused the deaths of thousands of people and the displacement of hundreds of thousands to other regions with the goal of finding better living conditions, causing serious economic, human and environmental disasters in the entire region.

In spite of the fact that these types of events and catastrophes have been coming about since the beginning and throughout human history, what we observe is that in the last decades this sort of events are happening more frequently each time and with wider repercussion around the world, probably, and almost no one escapes, that these disasters may be influenced with high probability by the new phenomenon of Globalization and climate change where the human actions carried out in one place have serious repercussions in other places or even in vast regions of the world (for example, Chernobyl in 1986 or Fukushima, Japan in 2011).

These facts would come to corroborate in some fashion the known Butterfly Effect which we spoke of earlier and that without a doubt have great importance for the majority of people and directly affects their jobs, their health, their lifestyle and their societies causing the word Change to become more relevant if fitting, until it turns into a "new paradigm" constant and permanent in our lives within a global environment in this common dwelling that we call our world. One of the most grave characteristics produced by Globalization today is the complexity that is generated within it and which may end up carrying tremendously disastrous consequences for the world as was seen in the previous financial crisis of 2008 where in spite of having the most sophisticated financial systems and the most qualified professionals of the banking system, no one saw it coming.

DEPENDENCE

It is estimated that 70% of basic or generic medications used by healthcare systems around the world are made in China. Production statistics from 2019 show that China is the premier producer of consumer electronics including, in this chapter, mobile phones, computers and televisions, assuming up to 85% of the global production of these products. China is the world's largest producer of rice and wheat and the largest producer and exporter of textile goods... add and continue... It is a fact that China is the largest country in the world by population, almost also by expanse, and it is certainly the largest producer in the world in such a way that it has become the world's factory in a little less than 30 years.

The process by which the country has reached its current predominant situation in numerous areas has not been exempt of difficulties and has been accompanied by a certain "bad reputation" for which many of its products have carried the label of "poor quality" for many years; although this situation is changing little by little and each time China is starting to produce higher quality products with greater added value, look at the 5G network, Lunar satellites, or the exponential growth of biotechnology.

Undoubtedly, the largest country in the world by population and production is called to be, or better said, already is, a great player within the economy, commerce and world politics and surely within no time will be, without a doubt, first at nearly every level. This new predominant position on the international stage will bring and in fact is already producing important consequences for the rest of the countries, many of which probably may not be very positive, rather more likely negative and quite harmful.

The most flagrant and visible case at our disposal suffered by the majority of countries is the Covid-19 pandemic and this is what we want to refer to when we talk about dependence; how is it possible that a great part of humanity was dependent and I would say almost pillaged of such an essential right as health by the dominant position of one country that holds 70% of medications and specifically respirators, masks and necessary tests as has been seen in this latest crisis? How have we reached this point? Who is responsible for such great negligence, that Governments have abandoned their duties? Frankly, this fact seems as relevant to us as leaving the lives of thousands of people in the hands of only one country as if the rest of the countries did not have a Ministry of Health. In the end, we think that history and votes will give notice to this great negligence in the majority of countries and Governments.

When we talk about Dependence with a capital D we refer precisely to what we have just evoked. It is not the same for a country to be dependent on petroleum, wood or any other natural resource than on the most essential and greatest priority as is the health of its citizens.

By the way, China is a country that is greatly dependent on many natural resources essential to the production of most of its products, such as petroleum, natural gas, steel, cotton, or corn... nevertheless, and as a consequence of Globalization, they have known how to weave a wide net for supplying these assets in a multitude of countries, primarily in Africa and in South America in exchange for huge capital investments and technical and human resources, knowing how to negotiate with local governments and at the same time assuring themselves of regular supply fountains by leveraging their economic predominance and at the same time availing themselves of an important political influence in each region they operate in.

These facts and China's predominant position in the world directly affects and in a crucial manner what we call "The Supply Chain"; that is to say, China is not only the world's number one producer, but also the world's largest Transporter; China possesses the largest fleet of merchant ships and the most extensive maritime transportation network in the world. How can this circumstance affect the rest of the world? It is not difficult to imagine that when a textile business, electronics company or automotive manufacturer in Spain, France or another country needs the necessary components to assemble its finished products and those come from China, Vietnam, Indonesia or some other Asian country, these travel in the majority of cases under a Chinese flag, we mean to say with their fleet of container ships and cargo.

It is true that other important European and Korean maritime transportation companies exist which play an important role in the international trade of merchandise, but China continues to have the upper hand with an additional advantage that is, and here as well, the predominance held by its ports at the time of loading and unloading for merchandise with the dominant position which recent times have been able to prove stemming from the Covid-19 crisis when shipments of goods were blocked for weeks in its ports, gravely affecting normal traffic and production in many countries.

When we speak of Dependence, we refer to all that which we have just enumerated and it is evident that China's position of dominance affects many countries and distorts the equilibrium and the normal unfolding of the world economy in the era of Globalization. Is there a solution for correcting this situation?

In our judgment, yes there is and it is called Diversification; that is to say, instead of depending on a sole provider (China) Supply Chains must be diversified by taking production to other countries on a development track that are thrilled to count on new production opportunities and future new clients resulting in the progress and wellbeing of its citizens. This will make it so that Supply Chains are not interrupted or disrupted by the dependence on a sole provider.

RULES AND VALUES

In this day and age, commercial relations and the economy in general no longer function solely between two or three countries like bilateral relations; that was then; today relations and international traffic are established among various countries and regions at the same time weaving a complex network independently among them; today relations are basically multilateral. What happens in one country may affect not only the other country with which they have established trade relations, but also other countries which are more or less connected with the first two countries, given that in the end all countries are connected in one way or another.

Actually, all countries and nearly all the products that are manufactured compete on a single "playing field", in a single market which is the Global Market. So that the products offered or sold in that single market may be offered in an equal and just manner, or in other words, in equal competition up against each other, certain rules and conditions are needed which must be arbitrated by a single arbitrator which in this case is the World Trade Organization (WTO) headquartered in Geneva, Switzerland. On the contrary, and to utilize a soccer simile, in a soccer match if the referee does not referee well, or allows himself to be influenced by one of the two teams, or worse still, abandons his duties, or lastly, as happens occasionally, the match is played without a referee, then the match and the result will have little value and will not be very fair nor will it reflect the reality of what transpired on the field of play, with the prejudice that it would bring for the players or for one of the two teams.

The previous example is completely valid today since in spite of China, in this case, the economic and social landscape has made great achievements, raising a great part of the population out of poverty and generating millions of jobs for its citizens; this achievement, would not have been possible without the low production costs of tens of thousands of goods exported around the world and without the minimally required sanitary conditions and protection of its millions of workers.

Besides, almost all consumers in many countries have been able to frequently prove the poor quality and lack of safety of many of their products, not to mention the irregular practices employed in their sales and marketing techniques. Although it is true that this situation is gradually improving due to the ever more exhaustive and regular controls that the authorities or the "Referees" are imposing with the end goal being that the result of the match between the competitors on the playing field be as equitable as possible.

These situations of disloyal competition which have been coming about for various decades on various playing fields, that is to say the markets, have some very harmful consequences for one or several of the contenders as no one would understand, to once again use the example of a soccer match, that one of the teams could win the match using their hands to play when the game is played with the feet, kicking constantly, making foul plays that the referee does not see or straight up playing without a referee, it is evident that the result of the match will be in favor of the team that has not respected the rules and very harmful to the team that has played by the rules.

The consequences for the teams (countries) that have played by the rules have been seen, in recent years, in many countries, corporations and their workforce that have lost competitiveness and have been forced to shut down as a result, causing the mass layoffs of thousands or workers who have lost their jobs to the outsourcing of production or even the subcontracting of other companies and their workers in countries with lower costs. Thus, preferring to play by a more relaxed set of rules, with the end goal of becoming more competitive or simply subsisting in a very dynamic global market. If the game is the same for all, the rules should also be the same for all.

WINNERS AND LOSERS

Colonialism has been over the centuries, after slavery, the most unjust and degrading form of exploitation by some men over others, or more specifically, by some rich countries over other poor countries. Colonialism is the manner by which one country appropriates another, either by force or with consent with an end to appropriating their resources, assets, people and which is then called a colony.

Historically, colonialism properly began in the 15th century with the discovery of America by part of the Spanish Crown with the implementation of the Viceroys, later continuing in other parts of Asia and Africa and it was in the 19th century when it takes a new impulse and accelerates with the intervention of other nations such as England, France, Portugal, Belgium, etcetera… reaching a dominance of a great part of the world.

This brief introduction serves us to better analyze the phenomenon of Globalization and its consequences. In effect, to our understanding, we ask if the actual phenomenon of Globalization may not be, keeping our distance obviously, a new form of lightly veiled colonization, but at the same time more subtle, through which the new large multinational corporations and almost all of us have the same ones in mind, may be appropriating in a more quiet and gradual manner our assets, our means of production, our culture and our societies, with the same end in mind as the old colonial empires. If we take the value of any corporation among the so called, "BIG Four", their value is almost the same as the Gross Domestic Product (GDP) of Spain or of other similar countries, more than a billion dollars.

The immense power that only these corporations have in this day and age makes various countries tremble and double over, including a certain block of countries: Recently, the European Union (EU) was forced to return the sum of 13 billion dollars to the Apple corporation as a refund of taxes withheld by way of a ruling in their favor from an EU Tribunal.

It may escape someone to think that these types of actions are not a new form of colonialism by which a large corporation brings an entire institution such as the EU to its knees?

What power have these large corporations managed to accumulate in order for these types of things that remind us, at least in an imperceptible manner, of old practices of subjugation and dominance under new means? Coming up we shall move on to explaining why the phenomenon of Globalization has created and continues to create a great polemic around the world.

In 1944, even before the end of World War II, the famous Bretton Woods Accords (Massachusetts, USA) set the basis for the foundation of the three most important economic bodies: The International Monetary Fund (IMF), The World Bank (WB) and The World Trade Organization (WTO); whose mission is to palliate the grave effects brought about by periodic crises, while at the same time promoting global economic development between countries with the goal of eradicating poverty and the misery generated by wars and cyclical crises. Nowadays, there is no doubt of the value and benefits that these institutions have developed since then in innumerable countries and by extension in almost all the world; notwithstanding, their actuation has not been exempt from controversy in numerous cases and in some countries their errors in the applied politics have been harmful and even nefarious, above all in the case of the IMF.

In the example we mentioned at the beginning of the chapter about the worker who loses their job in Europe in favor of another worker in a far off Asian country we can observe one part, perhaps the most painful, of what is happening with Globalization, although, as we said, this process does not limit itself to the freedom of movement of workers, instead it also deals with the liberalization of capital, patents, investments, projects and culture between different countries. These movements and displacements of the distinct assets and economic assets have had a considerable influence in the development and progress of many countries and possibly, one that has benefited most is China; ahead, we will explain why. By the same token and in some cases, some countries have not emerged as beneficiaries of the aforementioned politics, they have emerged seriously harmed; from there as we already said, stems the great discontent existing among various segments of the population and in certain regions of the world with what is happening.

Within the group of countries that have benefited the most from Globalization we could mention China, as we have already said, several East Asian countries, like Indonesia, South Korea, Vietnam, etcetera… some other African nation such as South Africa, Ghana, etcetera… Notwithstanding, a numerous group of countries on the American continent, like Argentina, Bolivia, Ecuador, Colombia… have not come out as well positioned and have suffered during decades of stagnation and even regression from which they struggle to emerge even now as a result of the bad politics applied both intermittently as well as by International Bodies, especially the IMF.

As Adam Smith said in The Wealth of Nations, "market forces act in such a way that in the end they always lead to equilibrium" driven by some sort of "invisible hand" that takes care of it in the end. Unfortunately, these forces only function and not entirely, in well informed markets and with almost perfect competition; but on the contrary, function quite differently in poorly informed, poorly regulated markets, lacking in protection of property and laws, as is the case in many developing countries. These existing conditions there, most often prevent applied politics from obtaining the expected result; instead, more often than not, they produce the opposite effect.

With a concrete example we will be able to get a better idea of what we discussed. In 1997 the devaluation of the Baht (national currency) in Thailand had repercussions that were felt throughout the region and affected numerous neighboring countries, provoking what came to be known as the "East Asian Crisis" during that time.

The recession created by this situation was originated and accelerated by the bad politics applied almost exclusively by the IMF, whose prescriptions have not varied much and it could be said that they are almost standard for all countries, regardless of their situation and their specific stage of development. Basically it consists of applying the radical liberalization of capital, often speculative, a rise in the types of interest rates for controlling inflation, and a strict plan of control over the conditions for aid and repayment of loans granted.

Another paradigmatic case is that of Argentina who in the last great crisis of the "Corralito" in 2001 saw itself forced to ask the IMF for help in order to emerge from a grave economic and financial situation in which it saw itself immersed due to the heavy debt it had incurred in recent years. Here, in the same manner and with the same prescription, the politics of the IMF were applied once again, control of exchanges, price control, draconian debt reduction and its conditions, etcetera, which accelerated a rampant recession and a great exodus of capital. The curious thing about the case is that Argentina's situation had little to do with that of East Asian countries, but nevertheless, the IMF once again applied the same tactics, exacerbating and further incrementing the recessions in both cases.

We could cite various examples more along the same lines, but we've chosen to cite these two for the relevance they played in their day during their respective crisis.

At the margin of intervention by international bodies in developing countries, the true causes and those truly harmed by the phenomenon of Globalization are primarily owed to the unbalanced relationship between developed countries and developing countries.

The principal causes, in our view, are several:

- On one hand, the existing differences in the terms of exchange; the price of products. Frequently, food products in general, which rich countries sell to poor countries, are subsidized by those countries' own governments, thereby creating unfair competition against local products.

- On the other hand, rich countries make sure to impose tariff barriers and rates for products imported from poor countries, forcing the latter to throw open its borders, putting the brakes on possible development and their takeoff, since they are unable to sell their products to rich countries.

- They impose harsh norms and legislation, especially sanitary conditions, in order for poor countries to sell their products in those markets.

- In some cases, rich countries install their own companies in poor countries with greater means and better technology creating unfair competition against local companies and driving many of them to close.

- The deficiencies in the active legislation in those countries and their weak regulation of the legal system and the norms, are additional advantages for large foreign companies installed there.

- Finally, and as we have said, the politics applied in these countries by the international bodies have been frequently erroneous, when not disastrous.

Based on what we have just commented on, we may observe that when we talk about Losers we are referring to many countries that, having integrated themselves into the process of Globalization, have not always obtained the benefits they expected for having lower labor costs and more relaxed social and security conditions, or sometimes nonexistent; since that would supposedly make them more competitive and they'd have more advantages in the global market, a fact, that although in numerous cases this has been a reality, in many other cases it has signified a deterioration and regression for the development of those countries.

As far as the supposed winners are concerned, we should say that they find themselves between two camps, as much in affluent countries as in less affluent countries.

It is an evenly contrasted fact that the investments made by rich countries in poor countries by installing their factories and their technology in those territories has created a greater wellbeing and development in many areas through the creation of millions of jobs that would have been difficult to obtain by other means. We reiterate that the most relevant case is perhaps that of China with the installation of thousands of western companies and the creation of millions of jobs, but also the case of other countries, like Vietnam, Bangladesh, Thailand, Indonesia, in Asia or Morocco, Algeria or Senegal, in Africa.

Yet without a doubt, the great beneficiary of Globalization has been China. More than three decades have passed since thousands of European and American corporations decided to install themselves in China with an end goal of becoming more competitive in the Global market, basically propelled by much lower production costs and more lax norms in the work conditions of their workers. During the last 30 years, China has been exporting and selling its cheap and in many cases poor quality products to the world, through which they have created a structure such that they have been called "The world's factory" for a while now. The immense economic potential obtained in the last decades has been gained by way of a well planned strategy supported and financed by a not very democratic State, with third world labor legislation and with more than dubious commercial practices acting as unfair competition on numerous occasions.

However, China has been changing its strategy for a few years now and is going from making cheap products to manufacturing other more value added products and actively investing in the sectors of technology with a greater future such artificial intelligence (AI), the space industry and robotics, being the country with the most robots installed in the entire world. Of course, it has not set aside its political strategy implanting and allying itself with numerous countries in Africa and South America with a goal of securing its supply chain of the resources needed for its industry and political and strategic dominance of these regions in the world.

Undoubtedly, this new geostrategic disposition on the world board of countries is having and will have in the future some consequences that are already being noticed in other parts of the world like the USA and in Europe where the loss of economic and political influence which is moving toward the East made President Trump react by increasing tariffs and raising rates on Chinese products, wielding a new slogan of "America First" to counteract the increasing power exhibited by China in technology with 5G and the Huawei Corporation or the launching of satellites into space to cite just two recent examples.

Parallel to this, Europe is also seeing itself threatened by this growing Chinese economic power and is already starting to take measures with new legislation to stop the avalanche of investments and massive buyouts of European companies on the part of China. Not only are thousands or millions of jobs in jeopardy, but there is also a danger of the loss of a certain social, cultural and scientific power which are the identity symbols of Europe or America. Now, yes we do think that these changes are sufficiently relevant and represent a new threat to keep in mind for the workers, corporations, and the institutions of the West.

DEGLOBALIZATION

Since the 1980s there developed a flood of thousands of companies that decided to outsource their production, or part of it, to countries with lower costs especially towards East Asia, singling out China above other countries that also received great investments and a multitude of Western companies wanting to establish themselves in their latitudes.

As costs and workers' salaries began to rise, many companies began to realize that manufacturing in those countries, especially in China, was no longer as profitable and started leaving for other countries with lower costs and many began to reconsider returning home before facing the problems that were coming.

In particular, problems with the quality of many products began to stand out, to the point of affecting the brand image of many of them; of course the issue of rising costs was another important factor if not the most important, and finally the regularly emerging problems of the breaks in the supply chain caused primarily by errors and blockages in shipping, above all as we have been able to see in this last crisis of Covid-19, wherein many ports in China reached the point of collapse with the grave consequences that ensued in many companies in Europe, forcing many of them to suspend production temporarily in the face of lacking supplies as was the case for various automotive companies or even companies in the healthcare sector, in some cases forcing partial lay-offs.

Faced with these circumstances and owing to repeated situations of this sort that have been coming about since a few years back and faced with the loss of control that this fact has meant for many companies and institutions, hundreds of companies have decided to pack their bags and return to the country from which they came given that the risks that were happening continuously, on many occasions, endangered the very survival of the company. Let us not forget that the most dangerous things for any company are the lack of security and the loss of control over its operation and its destiny.

It is not strange then, that in the face of the various threats and risks mentioned previously that President Trump raised the tariffs and rates on thousands of products originating in China before the risk of unfair competition against American products, arriving at uttering the famous phrase "America first", although perhaps in parallel he may have also taken advantage of the opportunity to gain some political return ahead of the next election cycle.

Nevertheless, President Trump did not stand alone, various countries have also started to reconsider their position on the international global board, as has been the case of the United Kingdom with a favorable Brexit vote two years ago. Although the reasons may differ from those put forth by the American president, it is clear that England has also decided to close its borders primarily due to an overly generalized sentiment in the country of a loss of control, especially as it concerns immigration, likewise, a certain surfeit with the growing power of Brussels, Belgium, and also why not say it, before the rise of populism led by the United Kingdom Independence Party (UKIP) and the manipulation over the vote from a particular segment of the population that it exercised in the last Brexit voting. We could cite other examples like Hungary with its clearly anti-European president or even Catalonia with its separatist parties that think they will be better off outside of the EU block than in it.

If the start and acceleration of Globalization that began in the past century represented the tumbling of walls between countries, and of its physical and mental barriers, the beginning of this century is being characterized by the raising of new walls and of physical and political barriers among many countries. This phenomenon is emboldening a dubious sentiment of protection of citizens against the unknown and at the same time a distrust and fear of "the others" which is very negatively influencing the normal operation of many countries and at the same time is being taken advantage of by certain politicians to save themselves and embolden a radical nationalist sentiment.

Things being thus, the great benefits generated by the process of Globalization from its beginnings are being harmed and halted in a notable manner by this backwards turn that some countries have decided to make and which from our point of view signifies a regression and an important recoiling for the natural operation of Globalization and its benefits in all the world.

GLOBAL GOVERNANCE

It has been some time, since the 19th century, the world is no longer a group of kingdoms nor of isolated and independent countries each living behind closed doors and trying to protect themselves from their neighbor or other countries further away. Nowadays and through the process of Globalization almost all countries live in only one world and in the same global house or in one global market, although each one maintains their customs and traditions. If this process has generated anything, it is precisely a standardization in the habits, mentality, tastes, and daily life of the global population. This has been provoked in part by large multinational corporations and the imposition of their rules, norms and fashions, and in another part by a group of countries that have decided and have seen the benefits of joining together in blocks or regions as is the case of the EU in Europe, Mercosur in South America, or Asia-Pacific in Asia.

As tends to happen in markets, together they have more power than they do separately. In this sense we want to remember that when we talk about rules and values, that since the majority of countries play on the same camp and on the same playing field, it seems logical and reasonable and I would say even demandable that they all be subject to the same rules so that the result of that "game" may finally be the most just, beneficial and equitable possible.

However, for this to be possible, the existence of an Arbitrator and a common Judge is necessary to conduct the game and apply the rules that will guarantee its propriety and "fair play" from start to finish and be accepted by all. In this sense, I would like to reference the reflection of George Soros in his book, "The Crisis of Global Capitalism" in which he notes that for a global and open society to adequately function it is necessary that the participants accept and commune with the same principles of a just society and always watching the social wellbeing of the majority.

It is not possible to leave the development of the game and the rules only in the hands of the "Market", since it has already been seen in previous crises, the individual interests or those of certain power groups upset and corrupt the democratic game producing the negative consequences and the enormous inequalities that we all know. In previous financial crises we have seen how the freedom of movement of capital and a certain adventurism by some financial groups have caused tremendous setbacks and disasters in many countries and in the global economic system.

For that, a new Global Body would need to be established that like the United Nations, which is in charge of regulating and conciliating the differences between countries at a political level, was responsible for dictating norms and suggesting the distinct regional Arbitrators so that the "game" of the global markets was proper and distributed the economic and social benefits of Globalization in a most just possible manner among peoples that form the Global Village.

CHAPTER TWO

WORK IN THE FUTURE

> *"Choose a job you like and you will never have to work a single day of your life."*
> *(Confucius)*

Of all the changes that have come about in society over the last century the change in work in all of its forms is probably the most relevant and also the most radical.

In his famous book, "The End of Work", the well known author and consultant to various governments, Jeremy Rifkin, advocates for the start of a new era and predicts that with the arrival of the fourth industrial revolution, millions of jobs are at risk and will disappear in almost all sectors leading millions of people, especially those who were among the last to incorporate themselves into the production process, to unemployment and a massive work stoppage; one need only to look at the unemployment rates of the majority of industrialized countries that had not been seen since before the Great Depression of 1929. This will bring, as a consequence, a division of the world into two most distinct forces: on one hand, the birth of a well-informed elite that will control and manage the global economy of

High Tech, and on the other hand, each time there will be a higher number of low qualified workers and with fewer guarantees of having a stable job with a future in a world that is more automated each day.

John Maynard Keynes, author of "The General Theory of Employment, Interest and Money" and without a doubt, the best world economist from the beginning of the past century already predicted that work time would be reduced in parallel to the rate at which the technological revolution would advance and make productivity grow in all sectors.

Most recently, Mexican businessman Carlos Slim, fourth richest man in the world, also said that the work week could be reduced to three days; and lately, businessman Jack Ma, owner of Alibaba, says that with the help of Artificial Intelligence (AI) the work week could be reduced to just twelve (12) hours divided over four days of the week…reality or fiction?? The truth is that these systems are already being employed in various countries like New Zealand, or even Germany with the "Teilzeit" because work hours are reduced to four days a week with the corresponding deduction to workers' wages.

Since the first industrial revolution started in the 18th century until the third industrial revolution, and soon the fourth will come, the evolution of work and of workers' social conditions have changed in such a way that nowadays talking about fourteen (14) and sixteen (16) hour workdays sounds prehistoric. In effect, when the steam engine was invented or the weaving looms in England, the workdays were regularly twelve to fourteen (12-14) or sixteen (16) hours and this circumstance varied very little until well into the 20th century. They were extenuating workdays and surrounded by unhealthy work conditions and in many cases dangerous for workers, since the main objective was to produce as much as possible, so that on one hand, they could amortize important investments of capital and machinery, and on the other hand, to try and get ahead of the competition with the end goal of obtaining more competitive products.

At the start of the 20th century the system mass production or production chain was introduced with the Taylorism Method of time and cost control, which allows the almost exponential multiplication in production of industrial and consumer goods, with the application of the scientific method of production and the creation of cost accounting. It is at this time that Unions arise to protect and defend the rights of workers who were frequently exploited by some businessmen with scant social sensibility. As Unions begin to grow in power, they begin to expand from England and the USA, where they were born, to other countries in Europe and the Americas arriving at the formation of an important social force to be taken into account by the majority of governments.

It is precisely, in the mid 20th century when the first computers or calculating machines appeared, and with the eruption shortly thereafter of information technology and forms of communication, Internet, mobile phones, etcetera…known today as IT that things start to change in a radical way substantially changing the ways of work, the norms that govern it and the interpersonal relations between workers and business owners, to finally arrive at the current situation in which we can see the enormous loss of Union power and the increase in power of those who hold the industrial capital, by this we understand it to mean, machinery, systems, information and processes. Each time, Capital gains more importance and the Work factor goes on losing relevance.

As a consequence of all these changes produced mainly by technological progress in distinct areas in the last century, the new working reality, and of the workers has little to do with those past times. Today is already a new reality that the jobs for life are no longer jobs for life, but instead for only a few years or a few months; that work contracts are no longer fixed, but rather temporary, that 8 or 9 hour days have turned into part time days, that each time more is spoken about a contract by project than about a contract for a position, that the term "freelance" or independent contractor is ever more popular, that it is no longer necessary to go into the office to work, instead one can telecommute, that you no longer need to go to or listen to a conference instead we can follow along at home on our monitors via an application (app); finally, companies are no longer those stable and immovable institutions as in the past where if you got into one of them it was for life; (Japan is a good example of this).

The new reality that is imposed and challenges us each day is that companies, jobs and institutions in general are no longer fixed, stable and durable, rather what is imposed and what forms part of our day to day, is Change, instability, flexibility, the availability to change jobs, companies, region and country when the situation calls for it. If we are capable of moving forward with this new mentality and way of looking at life and jobs, we will have plenty of control over our immediate future; on the contrary, we could see ourselves caught up in a whirlwind of events and new realities that we will not understand and which will prevent us from living better and seeing more clearly our place in this new and complex world full of technology in which we have to live.

TECHNOLOGY, ROBOTS AND DIGITIZATION

Without expressly referring to one of the most futuristic books, which has had the most influence over several generations, as is "Brave New World" by Aldous Huxley, we wanted to mention since the Utopia, or better yet, Dystopia, that the author proposes over a future happy society, we believe to be totally pertinent in the actual context of our own society.

In effect, the thesis proposed by the author in his futuristic novel is that for a society and its citizens to arrive at being completely happy, it is necessary that said society be controlled by certain castes (the most advanced and the most informed), in a way that the rest of the castes, that is to say, all of the other citizens, be regulated and controlled by those few ruling classes. The central idea is to achieve the highest level of happiness for the citizens and this will be achieved by way of constantly fomenting the desire to consume which in spite of being painful at first, in the end will provide pleasure by way of the purchased assets.

This would be made entirely possible by the total control of technology that would inundate practically everything, from leisure, with virtual games, even artificial human reproduction passing on to transportation through the cities in flying cars; all of the assets and products needed by that society would be produced by automated systems and machines, in such a way that the majority of society would dedicate its time to leisure and the development of hobbies or to pleasure which had also been envisioned through the use of a legal drug called "Soma" which would also take care of producing a permanent feeling of happiness and well-being in the citizens. At its core, the book is an acid critique of the capitalist and consumer society in which we live.

I make this reference, a bit extensive but totally relevant and timely, for our judgment, because in today's world technology is everywhere, inundating almost everything and we can almost say that it is everything. Technology has made humanity progress more in the last half century than in the previous twenty centuries combined. Breaking from this irrefutable reality, and without entering into philosophical considerations or of a different nature, it is not strange that evolution and the greatest demand of new jobs is intimately linked to technology. We can ask ourselves the why of that obsession for technology in the latest times; in reality, human beings have always looked for new ways of production and making things in less time and in a less costly manner with the goal of dedicating more time to leisure and family, or to put it another way, has sought to make more with less and at its core that is called increasing productivity which is what modern societies are all about.

Technology is the new goddess of the day whom everyone wants to worship; we want to manifest the influence she has had and has on work, on processes, and on employment in general.

With the invention of the steam engine in 1769, began a period where the majority of manual labor which up until then had been carried out by animals or humans was substituted by the mechanical power of machines, leaving thousands of horses and people who performed that work until then out of a job; some more of this occurred with the introduction of these machines in the textile industry which up until then had also employed thousands of people to the point where one textile mill that required the work of ten people at a time was reduced to employing only one or two people at the most.

The 19th century continued with the previous industrial revolution, improving the machinery created in the 18th century and introducing another important innovation as was the railroad; this improved nearly all transport systems and brought a wide range of jobs for the machinery industry bound for the metallurgical sector as well as other sectors, including manufacturing improvements in the machinery industry itself for the manufacturing of machines for multiple uses.

Then in the 20th century the internal combustion engine, gas turbines and electric motors were born that have innumerable uses in the manufacturing of home appliances, automobiles and later on trains, airplanes, etcetera. Everything changes with the arrival of the first programmable computer invented by Konrad Zuse in the 1940s during the past century, subsequently followed by IBM, Apple, etcetera. In 1983 the Internet was born at the United States Department of Defense with the creation of the Advanced Research Projects Agency (ARPA) and the fourth industrial revolution with the introduction of the World Wide Web (WWW), of IT and with the application of new programmable automated systems and AI, that extend to practically every sector turning most tasks and work into completely programmed and automated operations, significantly reducing the need for the human factor in work. This is without a doubt the principal Change that has come about since the middle of the last century and the beginning of this century and whose main consequence has been the creation of a new society almost completely automated in its daily endeavors and at the same time the destruction of millions of jobs and of repetitive tasks with little value added in the entire world.

As we have previously said, technology has become the new rising stock and we still do not know how to calibrate its future repercussions on society. Nevertheless, next we talk about three technologies that have completely changed the current world of work and labor relations in areas such as: robotics, AI, and digitization.

Within the new programmable automated systems, robots are, without a doubt, the stars of this sector for their wide range of uses in nearly every sector from agriculture, industry, medicine, transport to tourism. The implications that the introduction of this new technology has on questions of savings and productivity for the economy and for employment are almost infinite. It is almost unnecessary to provide examples; we have all seen at some point what a robot does on an automotive assembly line or on the paint section of that line, or how many parts of a clock a robot can make with mathematical precision, or how many hundreds of pieces are manufactured by robots for the aeronautics industry or how many tons of wheat a harvester can collect in one day... the list would be endless. The consequences of this new form of production jump into view: on one hand, an increase in productivity which makes companies more competitive; and at the same time a reduction in fixed costs and variables, among which without a doubt, the most notable, is the reduction in the human factor and the rise in unemployment.

For approximately one decade and more recently there was talk of so called Digitalization and little by little it was introduced in many companies, Organizations and Institutions. With this new system of process simplification thanks to the Internet and to the massive introduction of new information and communication technologies (IT) the intended objective to reach is similar to that of automation. In effect, and thanks to the development of new and sophisticated algorithms much time and great costs may be saved in the undertaking of regular tasks or jobs, and client relations with the consequential benefit of time and cost savings for all parties involved, which in turn translates into an increase in productivity and competitiveness in wide sectors of society.

The same as when we talk about robotization, the most negative direct consequence will likewise be a rise in job loss and unemployment rates.

We will use only two examples of the consequences from what we have just mentioned.

In the first case, the paint robot "Dürr" is able to paint a car in a factory in just over sixty seconds, or sixty cars an hour. Instead, that same car painted by a laborer would take between seventeen and twenty hours… the production gain is clear, correct?

In the sphere of digitization if we want to go to the doctor, for example, for a consultation, the median time required between getting there and back, wait time in the waiting room, etcetera, could take us from and hour to an hour and a half depending on where we live; nevertheless, the same consultation done via telemedicine or videoconference would only take five minutes. The difference in savings in this case is also clear.

The conclusion we can make from the consequences resulting from the introduction of new digital automation systems at work and in our lives is that they provide us with an important time and cost savings by being less costly, but at the same time, the most notable negative consequence is that in that transformation and going from an antiquated system to a new one there is a significant number of unemployed and people who will need to reinvent and integrate themselves into this new environment, who are left along the way.

Unfortunately, there will always be a residual number of people whom whether due to age or to the inability of adapting to new circumstances will remain separate and sidelined and will have to take early retirement or get government assistance.

It is the price that must be paid for progress or as the economist Joseph Shumpeter said it is the creative destruction of the economy. Which does not mean that this group of people must remain entirely at the margin of society and only represent a burden for the State. Multiple exits exist to continue providing society and to the individual well-being via the incorporation of this collective to other distinct tasks of the classic eight hour job such as professional help to the disabled, coordinated assistance to the elderly, delivering voluntary training to disadvantaged and low income youth, getting involved with a Non Governmental Organization (NGO), or even the development of monetizable personal artisanal or artistic aptitudes that will provide personal and societal benefits combined.

THE NEW PROFESSIONS

For better or for worse, technology and technological progress impact our day to day and most importantly, they will impact our future as human beings and as a society, changing our customs, our habits, our way of thinking, our personal and professional relationships, our world view and our values.

As far as work and the different professions are concerned, for several decades now, a real revolution has been generated in the different activities of the manufacturing economy and of the service economy. Agricultural production has been radically transformed with the introduction of new machinery such as the tractor, new irrigation systems; planting and gathering with the large harvesting machines, modern disinfecting systems and new, flexible transportation vehicles that take crops from field to market.

In general, it has been the introduction of robots and AI in mass form which has likewise changed the means of production from large steelworks to automotive factories, passing through construction systems and the machine-tool industry; and if we talk about transport, autonomous aircraft and autonomous automobiles are already the new reality; with regard to services, travel agencies, tourism, and even law firms are being transformed by this new virus called technology that impacts everything.

As a consequence of the new landscape and of this new reality, many jobs and professions of the recent past have already become extinct or will cease to be relevant in the not too distant future.

Among the old professions jobs such as, Watchman, Telephone Operator, Welder, Bill Collector, Secretary, Salesman, Laborer, Shop Clerk, Receptionist, Porter, Transporter, Taxi Driver, Mailman, Cashier, etcetera, no longer have a future, and in general, neither does any job that involves a repetitive or monotonous task capable of being substituted by a machine or by AI.

Even still, if we move on to more sophisticated professions such as an aviation pilot, insurance agent, attorney, technical architect, doctor, banker, civil servant, etcetera, likewise these professions will also be affected, albeit in smaller measure, by technological change and the new digital economy.

The new professions that are coming are all of those linked to the internet environment and to the new applications (apps) for mobile phones, biotechnology and food security, those related to the implementation of AI in numerous sectors, all those having to do with clean and sustainable energy, and those focusing on attention and services to the elderly or to the leisure sector. In this way we can prove that the new economy is quite different from the previous economic system and represents a substantial Change, and therefore will need new abilities and new jobs that did not exist until now.

Within the new professions we may highlight:

- Digital Marketing Manager
- Digital Media Manager
- Android and IOS Application Developer
- Web Page Designer
- Big Data Analyst
- Search Engine Marketing (SEM) and Search Engine Optimization (SEO) for better positioning on the Internet
- Environmental Engineers
- Digital Communication Experts

- Virtual Reality Experts
- Developer of 3D Printed Organs
- Robot Operator
- Cyber Security Experts
- E-commerce Specialists
- Geneticist
- Client Relationship Manager (CRM)
- Nurse
- Social Assistants

Surely for many, making the transition from jobs in the old economy to the new roles required by the current job market will not be easy, but as the saying goes, no pain, no gain, and the majority of the active working population in all countries finds itself in a process of transformation and of change that demands getting with the program and reinventing oneself as soon as possible. It's a matter of survival.

EMPLOYEE OR FREELANCER

Seeing the evolution of work since the beginning of the last century through today, we observe relevant phenomena that somehow explain the situation of the current job market:

On one hand, the great transformation there has been in production systems caused by successive technological revolutions; this has made producing goods and services each time more capital intensive (machinery, robots, systems, software) and labor has become a less important factor; hence, each time there are fewer jobs, especially in industry; (one need only look at the evolution of unemployment rates in many developed countries).

On the other hand, and as a consequence of the preceding, each time there are more self-employed or freelance workers who participate in all areas of the new economy. As an example, in the United States, 35% of the labor force is made up of one of these workers, and in Japan, a country traditionally made up of large corporations and jobs for life, in the last thirty years, 25% of its workforce is also comprised of these new workers, that was said by the preeminent Management expert, Peter Drucker, they're the new workers of knowing or knowledge.

Foreseeably that will be the tendency in the near future: so to speak, each time there will be more freelance workers and fewer employees working for others. In front of this situation that is already a reality today, it would be fitting to ask two questions for those entering the job market and for those that are exiting the system or will soon be expelled:

The first question would be: Does it make sense for my future to continue looking for work at a company that does not guarantee me any job security? On the contrary, do I start offering my knowledge and services as a freelancer which also does not guarantee me any job security, but that at least I can control and where I would be my own boss?

The answer to this dilemma depends on two important questions that are fit to ask oneself: first, am I sure that there is a market need for my knowledge and the services I'm offering? Second, do I believe I have the character and endurance capacity required to be my own boss and withstand the uncertainties of the market? Once we have answered these questions in an affirmative or negative sense, then we can better plan our future. At the core, the answer to these vital questions is the same as choosing between independence and insecurity (Freelance) or dependence and security (employee or civil servant).

In my personal experience as an economist and corporate consultant, I have been on both sides. During one third of my professional experience, I have worked as an employee and as an executive at mid-sized and multinational companies, and in the remaining two thirds of my professional activity I have been a freelance corporate consultant, sometimes with employees and the majority of the time as an independent contractor. Anecdotally, I should say that within the services we offered in the corporate offices, one was the hiring of personnel; and I remember that in many interviews with candidates for a role, one of the questions I asked was: "What would you like to be or what position would you like to have in the future?" On countless occasions the answer of many candidates was "I would like to be a civil servant." When asked why, they systematically replied, "That way I'll have a stable job for life and they cannot fire me." Needless to say, in spite of a human being's inherent need for security, this type of candidate was filed under: "Not suitable for the job"; not because of their objective to become civil servants, but rather due to the motives they gave for occupying the post.

Looking toward the future, I believe that we're headed more each time towards a labor market where each one will have to sell their knowhow or what they are best suited for, that is to say, their talent.

Mass production and large corporations with thousands of employees will soon be a thing of the past or in any case will center on a few dominant organizations that will form oligopolies of the AGFA type: Apple, Google, Facebook, Amazon and those that manufacture mass consumer goods which will concentrate in developing countries with very low labor costs, but without much added value.

TALENT

We could define Talent as that special and different quality or ability possessed by people to fulfill a task in a specific field and what sets them apart from the rest by making something look easy that is difficult for others. Departing from this supposition, and understanding that what the market will ask for in the future is precisely people's Talent (routine tasks are already being done by robots), it is important and without delay for the majority of active people in the job market, to reflect profoundly on their best qualities and the most relevant knowledge at their disposal in order to be able to offer these to the market and to society. This introspective analysis will be particularly important for each person that wants to know what their employability index is and what their viable possibilities in the market of the new digital economy are.

What the market and corporations demand and will ask for in the future is the contribution of value or the best Talent each person has to offer, which is the same thing; we are moving toward a market of Experts; and to know and discover what is that special talent we possess there are various roads: one, is the retrospective analysis, that is to say, looking back and seeing in which jobs or activities we did especially well and we have had a certain amount of success or also review among our group of friends and work colleagues where and when we received praise for a job well done under given circumstances. Another way would be to revisit our years of education and recall some recognition received from a teacher in a specific subject or an award or some success that we may have achieved. The other road is to listen to the heart; or as Steve Jobs used to say, when faced with two roads from which to choose, always choose the one dictated by your heart.

Two examples of what we have just commented on would be: in one of the films starring the actor Sylvester Stallone, where he plays a boxer, his character says, "I was born for this", also the famous tennis player, Garbine Muguruza in one of her interviews said to the journalist, "I am tennis" or even the famous American actor Al Pacino tells how a high school teacher told him that he was destined to become a good actor.

In this sense, and so that everyone may do their own internal analysis in search of their Talent, I would recommend two books: the first is "The Element" by Ken Robinson, probably the most knowledgeable person in the field of education and in which he recommends that every person ought to have a tutor; the second is "Archeology of Talent" by Alberto Sanchez Bayo, economist, coach and talent archeologist.

The three qualities that will be most in demand by today's market and in the future are: continuous improvement, resilience and flexibility.

OPPORTUNITIES

If we observe what has happened in the labor market of many countries during the last decades we can see that the rise in unemployment and joblessness, above all in certain sectors has not stopped growing. Is this a consequence of the massive introduction of technology to all areas of the economy? I believe denying it would be like living in another world; that is to say, joblessness and the rise in unemployment have been a true and direct consequence provoked by the generalized introduction of new technologies in this new era which we have entered, called the "fourth industrial revolution". In spite of it, according to estimates of some economic organizations, in Europe there are one million job openings waiting to be filled since there are not enough especially qualified workers in existence to fill them, above all in the new digital economy.

This new reality is particularly relevant in industrialized and more technically advanced countries; however, we think this phenomenon will still take a few decades to manifest in developing countries, since many of these countries still find themselves in the second or third industrial revolution and many opportunities exist in those markets offering thousands of jobs requiring medium to high level qualifications. To this purpose, I would like to share a real and personal anecdote that happened to me a few decades ago.

When I completed my studies in economics at a European university and having obtained my degree as an economist, I and a classmate began our job search by sending hundreds of letters to multinational companies and other international organizations of which the country in question had plenty. The result after a few months of intense searching was fruitless; the most numerous replies were of the type: "we need candidates with experience" or "as you know, we are in the midst of an economic crisis and a hiring freeze, we're sorry". We must not forget that 1974 was the year of the great oil crisis, wherein the oil producing Arabic nations decided to quadruple the price of oil overnight, which brutally affected every economy in the world.

As things were and following weeks of reflection, and faced with a lack of prospects, I took a world map, put my finger on a South American country (an oil producing nation) and that is where I went to try my luck: after one month and some negotiating and some contacts, a consulting firm selected me for the position to manage a midsized metallurgical company.

There I was at 25 years of age and taking charge of a company with 80 employees of various nationalities and with the responsibility of driving into safe harbor a ship that was in relatively good condition. Needless to say that in the first months, the stress and anxiety stemming from the lack of experience made their presence known almost daily, but as a good navigator (I have been navigating for 40 years), I managed to make it with that vessel and its crew. After a time, I received an offer from an American multinational corporation to head their financial department, which I accepted as I thought it meant a considerable improvement in my career and working conditions. I remained there for several years, until after seven years in that country and seeing the drastic political changes that were coming, we decided as a family to return to Spain.

I have shared this personal anecdote because I consider it relevant for thousands of young graduates or qualified professionals for whom, under given circumstances in Europe, it is difficult to find work or a position suitable to their qualifications. When I speak of opportunities, I am referring to real opportunities that radically change work prospects and the future of many young people in old Europe. Also, we must add that those coming from Europe are well thought of and valued. The only obstacle is fear; and one must learn to manage it.

TELEWORK

Another of the changes, and not the least important, that has brought about the technological transformation of which we speak is Telework. This new modality of working and productivity for companies, is not really all that new, I have personally been teleworking for twenty years and providing service to clients, but it has seen itself incremented and accelerated by an important event as is Covid-19.

This has meant a radical change for many companies upon discovering that many of the functions that were previously performed on site could be performed from a distance and without a physical presence in the building. For the time being, the majority have found that in the face of fear of losing control of their workforce and the false idea that it may cause a loss of control and productivity that would directly affect the corporate yield, they have been able to prove after several months of practice, that it has not only affected the corporate yield but rather it has been incremented in notable fashion by reducing various fixed and variable costs in a significant way, such as office rent, transportation and energy costs of its employees, as well as the structural costs of materials, devices, office equipment, and other costs derived from the waste of thousands of hours in commute times.

At the same time, this change in the way of working has meant a significant improvement in general quality of life for thousands of workers, allowing for coveted family time to be possible for example, on top of representing an improvement in the physical and mental health of many workers by considerably diminishing the stress derived from long hours and commute times as well as a physical improvement due to a reduction in pollution that these displacements bring about. No less important, likewise is the improvement in the individual sensation of being your own boss and having more control over your time and personal life.

Obviously, alongside these positive aspects, many workers have experienced a variety of sensations and new emotions like a certain isolation and feelings of loneliness, the loss of coffee breaks and shared breakrooms, less social interaction with colleagues and some have even commented, the longing for in person meetings where aside from sharing in the atmosphere and company culture they have also missed the sharing of new and innovative ideas which, in contrast to virtual meetings, appear to come more easily and organically during in person meetings. Physical contact continues to be important as we are still social beings.

Some of these inconveniences have been resolved in a rather efficient manner by the massive employment of new technologies such as the Zoom or Skype platforms for interviews and meetings, and with other more commonly used tools such as email, WhatsApp, mobile phones, scanners and other proprietary communication apps specific to some companies.

The new digital economy with all of its novel mediums is here to stay and we believe there is no turning back, quite the contrary, as we advance in innovations and develop new devices and new applications, the economy, workers, and companies will suffer a transformation such that within a few years they will not resemble anything like the ways of work and production that we have known until now.

Hence, we think that Telework brings many more benefits than losses to companies and workers. The company of the 20th century with massive structures and thousands of workers at its locations is dead, save for clearly in certain areas of mass production.

What is coming is the Freelance worker, the worker with know how and the Expert who sells their knowledge and services to an ever increasing number of firms or institutions.

REINVENT OF RECYCLE

The consequence of all these changes introduced by technological innovation in recent times forces us to frequently reflect on our life and our circumstances and to reassess how our future will be at work, with family, and in our social relations, once we have suffered the consequences of these changes.

The words recycle and reinvent have come into fashion in recent times and although for many of us it is still quite difficult to understand the true meaning of these expressions, there is no doubt that they have become words similar to the warning lights on a car when something has gone wrong.

In one delicious little book published in 2012 by the Catalan philosopher Antonio Fornes, entitled "Reinitiate", he analyzes and reviews the lives of various famous and illustrious men in history (Kant, Pascal, Gaugin, Voltaire, etcetera) that demonstrates how these men changed the course of their lives and in some cases changed the course of history by having discovered their talent and true vocation and how they broke with their past and old profession facing their fears and their families to dedicate themselves to that which motivated them most and which they believe to be the occupation for which they were destined and through which they could provide more value to society. That is how Kant went from being a prestigious lawyer to one of the most important philosophers in history; Gaugin traded in his old profession as a stockbroker on the Paris Stock Exchange to dedicate himself in body and soul to his vocation as a painter becoming one of the most outstanding impressionist painters, and so on.

Almost all of us have experienced one or several personal crises at some point in our lives in which we have felt that we were not on the right track of our chosen path or even when an exceptional circumstance such as getting fired from a job, or facing a business or professional failure, has shaken us and has made us think and reflect that perhaps if we change course or dedicated ourselves to something else we would be better off and would be more satisfied.

What has changed in the last decades is the speed and regularity with which change happens at all levels, making personal and social crises more frequent each time and making it harder to understand what is going on. That is why there has been an exponential growth of self help books to solve those personal crises on one hand, and on the other hand, a proliferation of master classes of all sorts and in every field trying to bring many people up to date who have yet to find their true direction.

As we said in the previous sub-chapter speaking of Talent among the most in demand qualities of the future will be continuous improvement and constant learning.

CHAPTER THREE

THE NEW ECONOMY

"No society can surely be flourishing and happy, of which the far greater part of the members are poor and miserable."
(Adam Smith, The Wealth of Nations, 1776)

"Economics is the social science that deals with the best assignment of the scarce resources existent in the world to satisfy an unlimited demand." This definition, among others, reflects quite well what economics deals with or what it consists of. Actually and in some time periods this affirmation may seem a paradox, especially in times of crisis where demand and consumption fall drastically and what we have is an excess on offer as we are seeing in this recent crisis in which there is an excess of cars, petroleum, airline seats, hotel rooms…

In the past the economy centered above all on the extraction, production, distribution and sale of the majority of the existing resources. Nowadays, when we talk about the new economy we refer to a new reality reflected in expressions such as circular economy, digital economy, green economy, sustainable development, etcetera. These terms are not only a new fad to refer to the actual state of things, but rather expressions that define the new reality of the economy that runs parallel with the traditional economy to produce, transport, distribute and sell.

At the dawn of humanity and during many centuries men were basically hunter gatherers and it was not until the inception and establishment of agriculture and livestock in ancient Mesopotamia that the human being, once settled and stable, began to recognize the value of the things produced by way of trading agriculture products and selling livestock in exchange for other products with other people. It was that consciousness of property and trade value that gave birth to the traditional economy that persisted throughout the centuries and was the root of wealth for many countries, until the Middle Ages when the figure of the Artisan appeared and was imbued with value in the most diverse branches. Afterwards, in the 18th century, the first industrial revolution begins with the production of the first machines that accelerate and enormously increment productivity in the economy, together with the expansion of international commerce that grow in the 19th century with the mass production of all types of machinery, railroads, etcetera, and it is in the 20th century with new inventions, technological expansion and with the beginning of Globalization, when the highest levels of production are reached and well-being for a great part of the world population.

However, it is in the 21st century of which we have only covered one fifth thus far, when innovation, research and development of the most sophisticated machines and devices and of the most varied technologies and applications that are having a revolutionary impact in the actual means of production, transportation and communication never before known to man, have literally shot out. From this new state of things at which we have arrived is born what we call the New Economy whose different facets we will touch on next.

DIGITAL ECONOMY

The digital economy is based on new technologies (IT) and utilizes them as an efficient new instrument to meet the needs of assets, services, communication and leisure of consumers in an immediate manner, shared and global. This is possible thanks to the Internet and the innumerable applications developed specifically for each sector.

The digital economy is a new form of production, consumption, information, and communication. It deals with a complex process that involves changes in social organization, economics and politics of countries and by itself represents an ecosystem based on an infrastructure of the networks of communication, processing services, and web technologies whose development and implementation contribute to the rapid development of countries. It is comprised of four key elements: the infrastructure of telecommunications, broadband networks, e-commerce, end users (people, businesses, governments, institutions…).

The most outstanding characteristics of the new digital economy are: the generation of knowledge on all sides via platforms such as Wikipedia (Universal Free Encyclopedia), immediate access to millions of videos uploaded daily to YouTube, the virtual conferences on the most varied topics (TED Talks), and real time communication between people and businesses through applications like Zoom, Skype, etcetera…

We all make and practice the digital economy daily when we send an email to a client or supplier or to a friend; when we transfer money from home without the need of going to the bank, when we order food or other items from the supermarket, when we make airline or hotel room reservations without getting out of our chair, when we watch a movie on our screen or when we attend a music concert virtually; when we have a medical consultation over our computer in a nearly in person way, and when we speak to or see our friends and family over WhatsApp or Facetime.

Adapting to this new form of digital economy is relatively simple between people, and as a matter of fact most of us practice it daily, where it acquires its true value and relevance is in its implementation in companies, Governments and institutions. It is here, where it is necessary to design real and efficient digital transformation plans so that its implementation delivers the beneficial results expected by society. For that we need to count on experts competent in the new technologies to help us in such an endeavor and it is not enough to say that one company or institution has gone digital for the simple fact of having said so or of having a preview plan to that effect.

Among the numerous benefits conveyed by adapting to the new digital economy are: immediate and nearly unlimited access to knowledge, to innovation precisely because of the collaboration and sharing of that knowledge, the immediacy applied to all processes, disintermediation by bringing the producer and the consumer together directly, and this has benefitted the Globalization; companies improve their processes and reduce their transaction costs, Governments improve their services to citizens and improve their transparency, and finally citizens dispose of better information and as such better choices in their decisions which improves the competition and productivity of companies.

On the negative side, it must be said that new technologies produce a digital gap among citizens that have access to these and those who do not have access or are not allowed in various parts of the world for instance; likewise this gap is made palpable among consumers used to this new digital reality and those that, due to age or other circumstances, have a more difficult time entering the new economy.

Another negative effect are the thousands of unemployed that are creating these new technologies and that are not easily recouped, increasing in this manner the unemployment numbers in numerous sectors and countries.

To try and diminish this digital gap among those who do not yet have access for different reasons and among the elderly for whom it is generally more difficult to get up to date it becomes necessary for Governments and other institutions to implement educational programs in the area of digital technology with the goal that the majority of the population will benefit from the positive results of digitalization. It is a question of justice and progress for countries.

CIRCULAR ECONOMY

In the traditional economy the life cycle of a product consists of its extraction, production, transport, final consumption and death of that product. It is a closed circle.

In the circular economy, that same product has various lives as it is a model that consists of sharing, reusing, repairing, and renewing existing products and materials as often as possible to create an added value, thereby extending the lifecycle of products. What are the consequences of adopting this model of production and consumption?

The benefits for the economy, for the environment and for society are huge given that the principle on which this new model is based manages to give various lives to the products we consume, producing an enormous savings (valued by the CEE at more than 600,000 million euros) with the reutilization of the 2,500 million tons of residuals generated by companies and households in the EU; this is equivalent to 8% of the volume of total businesses in the zone, on top of reducing between 2 and 4% of emissions to the environment. Additionally, this new form of manufacturing, reusing and consuming could generate up to 500,000 jobs in auxiliary industries that would be created as a result. Although the benefits of the model do not end there, the reduction that would result in the extraction of raw materials needed for production would generate additional benefits that would further preserve existing resources which are finite and likewise would help reduce the carbon footprint on the environment that would result from the extraction and transport of those materials.

The European Union is seriously invested in it by way of a series of programs and financial aid to propel this new economic model. In a study carried out also by the European Commission for Latin America it is calculated that 50% of residuals are organic matter, of which 90% is not used or goes in the garbage. According to this Commission, improving the efficiency and the useful life of materials in that region could lead to generating five million jobs.

In Germany and Japan the interpretation of the circular economy is based on the three Rs (Reduce, Reuse, Recycle), the idea is that the actual flow of materials (resource, product, residuals) must be transformed into a circular flow of: resource, product, recycled product.

With this new model of economic thinking various things are obtained as we have mentioned; on one hand the life of products is extended giving them various new lives, the exploitation of limited resources on Earth is curbed, and the quality of the environment is improved at least by limiting the use of hydrocarbons and fossil fuels and their progressive substitution with cleaner renewable energy.

We'll give the example of a global company known by everyone such as Apple. At Apple Robotics, they have at their disposal an iPhone disassembling robot with 29 arms that is capable of dismantling a defective iPhone in 11 seconds and separating its components into reusable materials. To date, with this robot, Apple has saved sixty million euros in reusable material for future products, including 1000 kg of gold with a value of nearly forty million euros in gold.

It is calculated that in industrialized countries, 30% of food ends up in the garbage. This is another example of how even residuals can enjoy a new life and be useful to the planet by way of their reutilization as biomass or organic material.

COLLABORATIVE ECONOMY

We may define the collaborative or shared economy as a relationship between private parties to complete transactions in the online market; sometimes, this exchange is done through an intermediary or a platform. In this way the consumer acts in a dual role, sometimes as a purveyor of goods or services and other times as a consumer. It is calculated that the collaborative economy actually transacts some 200 billion dollars a year. The reason and the finality of this new exchange system (bartering already existed in the middle ages) is that of giving and utilizing the true value of things, in many cases giving them a second or third life which benefits the owners of the assets as much as the consumers, thereby both emerge as winners.

As we have just said this exchange can be between private parties or via a platform (Uber, Ebay, Airbnb) where all sorts of goods and services may be exchanged, a car, a house, work, professional services, etcetera… Sometimes the term Uberization of the economy is used to inadequately describe this system of exchange because it was one of the first platforms to initiate the sharing economy. This has been possible and at the same time propelled by technological, economic, political, and social changes that have come about of late. The Web or Internet has transformed everything, the two great recessions that occurred in the last ten years have also influenced in a defining form the change in habits and the way citizens buy things, and finally the traditional model of consumption to use and throw away has also begun to be seriously called into question.

The central and propelling idea of this system is that "the value that is not utilized is lost value"; the consequence of this has led to the increase of collaborative consumption under one of its premises that says "what is mine is yours".

This new form of consumption and of doing things has provoked a disruptive change in consumption and in the economy whose end is not envisioned in the mid-term but rather it more likely announces an important increment of this new system and of this form of exchange in the future. It is calculated that the value exchanged by 2025 will reach 300 billion dollars, a volume of business that surpasses the GDP of many countries.

Among the benefits generated by this new economic model it is fitting to highlight the following:

- Reduces the negative impact on the environment by diminishing the quantity of assets produced, thereby reducing industrial pollution.
- Reduces consumer costs by recycling interchanged articles.
- Gives people access to assets they are not able to buy.
- Accelerates the patterns of consumption and sustainable production.

On the negative side, its primary consequences are:

- The loss of jobs and a rise in unemployment.
- Skirts the law in various aspects, above all with regard to the protection of workers.

- Favors a rise in new platforms and start-ups whose only objective is to benefit.

All of this leads to the consideration and implementation of a more sustainable economy.

SUSTAINABLE ECONOMY

The law of Sustainable Economy published in the Official State Bulletin on the 5th of March 2011 defines it as a pattern of economic growth and development, social and environmental in a productive and competitive economy that favors quality employment, equal opportunity, a guarantee of respect for the environment and the rationed use of natural resources.

In this sense, the mission of sustainable development is, in addition to producing, the protection of the environment through the use of renewable energy, the bet on efficiency and taking advantage of scarce natural resources, the promotion of recycling and the reduction in consumption, and finally, the rise in social well-being through education and innovation.

How is this achieved? Once again, the economic system in place until now was based on the growth and production of limitless assets and the time has come when we have observed that the resources of this world are limited and that the environmental damage provoked by this runaway train of growth and rise in GDP of countries has a limit that we are seeing daily in all societies and that takes us to a point of reflection, of stopping and starting again or to use electronic terminology, "rebooting" ourselves.

The objective of economies at a world level should not be from this moment on a crazy race to increase the Gross Domestic Product (GDP) in spite of knowing that it is an easy index that shows the progress of countries and thus they may compare one another in a sort of competition of sporting results, rather the goal to reach is, of course, increasing production, but in a sustainable way and less harmful for people, society, and the environment through the use of new techniques and cleaner processes and accords with respect to nature.

Until now, the objective of nearly all countries has been to increase the GDP, that is to say the quantity of goods and services; with the sustainable economy, quality is more important than quantity and that will be achieved through the development of politics directed at promoting the utilization of renewable sources of energy and promoting competitiveness of sustainable activities that will invest in the development of innovation and education.

To summarize, Governments have the obligation of favoring and promoting growth through appropriate politics, given that without growth there is nothing; but they are also obliged to promote the human and social development of the countries they lead with the goal of reaching better levels of well-being in health, education and security which is what will make society more just and egalitarian.

REAL ECONOMY

By Real Economy we understand the economy that extracts, produces, transforms, transports, communicates, sells and distributes the goods consumed every day by people in the entire world. In this regular and permanent exchange intervene people, companies, institutions and governments that make the rules and dictate the laws so that this exchange may be as just and egalitarian as possible.

We are no longer in the times during which Adam Smith who, propelled by his optimism and idealism said that thing about markets being so efficient that they self regulate and always tend toward a balance in prices, conditions, etcetera (The Wealth of Nations 1776). The actual economy is formed by other forces, in addition to the markets which are the principal actors; governments, big corporations, lobbying groups, cartels, banks and tax havens claim more power each day, to the point where actual markets conform to a largely distorted reality of that ideal market Adam Smith dreamed of.

When Maria goes to the market or the supermarket to do her weekly shopping she is practicing real economics as a consumer of a series of products that in order to be available on the shelves have traversed every facet of the real economy; that is to say, they have had to be extracted or gathered, manufactured, transformed, packaged, transported and distributed until reaching their destination, that is the consumer. This is real economics.

Real economics is also when a citizen decides to buy a home and by that decision an entire process is activated, from purchasing the flooring, the necessary permits, project design by an architect, construction of the structure using cement and steel sold by a supplier, the construction of the house with its different stages in which of course the following have been involved, construction workers, manufacturers of bricks, tile, windows, doors, glass, electricity, paint, plumbing, etcetera, until finally, when the house is finished it is delivered to the buyer who has surely also asked a bank for a loan and in the end has likewise liquidated the corresponding taxes. This is also real economics.

The real economy generates jobs andproducts, produces useful things such as food, vehicles, houses, machines, etc. and generates tax revenue which is much needed to maintain the states social well-being; as opposed to the financial economy which many times produces speculation and catastrophic bubbles as was seen in the last financial crisis of 2008 with its terrible consequences for people and society.

FINANCIAL ECONOMY

The financial economy is formed primarily by a few economic agents such as banks, private or public saving societies, the Stock Exchange, private lenders, public financial institutions like the Official Credit Institute (Instituto de Crédito Oficial, ICO), investment funds and pension funds, insurers, and more recently, venture capital funds, crowdfunding, etcetera. Within these financing mechanisms we must distinguish between those that are useful and necessary for the development of economic activity (banks, saving societies, the ICO, the Stock Exchange, etcetera) and those that are useless and even detrimental for the collective economy (certain investment funds, vulture funds, the futures market, the forex or money market, tax havens, or money derived from illicit activities).

Finances or legal money are the blood or the circulatory system of the economic body, that is to say the economy; framed here are the banks, lenders, public institutions, etcetera, that we have already mentioned. On the contrary, in the second group are certain so called vulture or high risk funds, the futures market with its swaps, ICF, short sales, etcetera, unknown to most citizens, the money market where the rate of exchange is speculated 24 hours a day and whose end is only to obtain a quick gain in each transaction without having anything to do with the real economy, or the immense casino that tax havens represent, completely legal and authorized by governments, where a game of betting on red or black is played each day with money that escapes any government control and which represents a world volume of close to 5 billion dollars according to some estimates.

Therefore, in this way, the world economy moves and pivots on two superimposed levels as in a two story duplex that are connected by a spiral staircase, but lead totally parallel and independent lives. In this manner, while the bottom floor, occupied by a kitchen, lounge, and work studio, leads a relatively normal life; the floor above, occupied by the bedrooms, focuses on rest and thinking of ways to create more work for the first floor.

Once in a while, on the floor above and due to the fact that its residents spend the majority of the time dedicated to leisure or resting, a flood or a leak of toxic material happens (bubbles, crises, speculation, etcetera) that suddenly erupts on the bottom floor causing great material damages and in its residents (the real economy, everyday people).

I have taken the liberty of using this virtual example to illustrate, at least by means of an approximation, what is happening daily in the world economy, that is to say that the interaction between the bottom floor (real economy) and the top floor (financial economy) continues to produce some imbalances, some maladjustments, and some inequalities for the citizens that are the root of the actual discontent and of the general frustration, above all of the youth, who upon seeing that the global house in which they live is not functioning correctly, primarily because the ones from the floor above (speculators, funds, power groups, politicians) are constantly throwing waste and toxic elements at those on the floor below preventing them from leading a normal life and exercising an enormous pressure that completely dominates those on the bottom floor who must endure their excesses. Warren Buffet, possibly the best financier in the world, already said that the financial economy of toxic products (futures, forex, etcetera) are weapons of mass destruction, capable of producing enormous irreparable damage.

The question then that we may ask ourselves is: How can the economy liberate itself from the tenants on the top floor that represent the financial economy so that they do not continue to disturb and harm the tenants on the bottom floor, those representing the real economy? This is precisely one of the primary functions of Governments, that is to say, to establish rules and regulations that monitor and control those dangerous tenants, through the use of sanctions and taxes that impede and disincentivize those actors from carrying out actions that can damage and seriously harm the real economy and everyday people.

I believe that the end goal of all society is to make the institutions function, that the rules and laws are applied, that efficient control is established over their application, that private property be respected, that the economy be allowed to function in an independent and efficient manner within a regulatory framework agreed upon by all. However, there cannot be social justice until there is economic justice, and the Government must also take care of this since its principal commitment is to provide the greatest well-being to the citizens.

THE DEBT

The world debt is composed of three principal actors: the public debt of countries, corporate debt, and consumer debt. According to the Institute of International Finance (IIF) the total world debt in 2019 rose to 255 trillion dollars (220 trillion euros)! Frightening, no? This is distributed in the following manner: 70 trillion dollars in Government debt; 100 trillion dollars in corporate debt; 85 trillion dollars in consumer debt approximately (among these are also counted the debts of banks to each other and that of banks with central banks). This panorama gives chills just thinking about it. What can be done? Will the economy on its own be capable of resolving this enormous problem through additional growth or other measures? Sincerely, we think not!

In the first month of the Covid-19 pandemic, the world debt grew by 2.5 trillion dollars against the .9 trillion dollars that it had grown by in the same month the year before. We can infer that in the following months and in what is left until the pandemic is over, the debt will soar in exponential form just by looking at the massive indebtedness programs that the central banks and the majority of Governments have implemented in an attempt to palliate and stabilize the enormous decrease in activity and international commerce in the entire world.

How do we get out of this? That is the million dollar question, as the saying goes. Carmen Reinhart, Director of the World Bank, has noted recently that both families and businesses will have a very difficult time emerging from this situation of indebtedness, given that the central banks may continue to print money as they are doing, for example, the Federal Reserve in the United States and nothing happens, since the public debt may be converted into perpetual debts, that is to say, that it is never paid off; on the contrary, businesses and families have it more complicated as we all know what happens when a debt goes unpaid: liens, lawsuits, foreclosures, refinancing, etcetera, the never-ending story, leaving in its wake thousands of economic cadavers and families and businesses destroyed.

Carmen Reinhart suggests a solution, at least a partial one, that could alleviate and help in some way to gradually overcome this situation by way of a "release", a dreaded word for banks and creditors, but that in an exceptional situation like the one the world is living in today, could be a way out of the immense problems and dramatic situations that the majority of social agents are experiencing.

By way of this solution, one part of the debt might be "forgiven" or erased, and the remaining portion may be refinanced with more reasonable conditions so that both businesses and families alike might begin to envision a more positive future.

At its core, this is what many Governments in the world do when from time to time they see themselves overcome by debt.

If we look closely at the international landscape we will see that many countries have big problems with debt, and we are not exclusively referring to developing countries. With just a glimpse at developed countries like Spain, Italy, Japan, the United States, and England, we will see that the future before fixing this pressing problem, is more likely uncertain.

Ten years ago, Spain had a public debt of 80% of the GDP, today it has a public debt of 120% above the GDP. England is around that level too, Italy is around 140%, the United States hovers around 110% and finally Japan, (laborious Japan) has a public debt of 250% above the GDP. The general consensus regarding the state of the public debt in a country is that it should be around 60%; this is what the Organization for Economic Cooperation and Development (OECD) recommends.

Once again we ask ourselves: Who fixes this? How has this unsustainable situation been reached, however it looks? How is it possible that the third most developed nation in the world, as is Japan, has a public debt of 250% of its GDP? Why does no one, no country or international forum talk about this? It is true that the most of this debt is internal, that is to say, it is held by the Japanese themselves, and in some ways it is less serious than an external debt, that which is owed to another country or to other citizens outside of your country; but it does not stop being an immense snowball that if the citizens of Japan suddenly decided to rescue their titles and cash in their public bonds, it could turn into a nuclear bomb for world finances.

At this moment in time, the world economy is immersed in a world debt crisis that if it were to explode, we estimate that it would be the worst of the capitalist system since its implantation. We must not forget that the majority of crises are produced either by an excessive rise of inflation or by an out of control increase in debt.

THE CARTELS

The four Oscar winning film, "Network" (1976) directed by Sidney Lumet and starring William Holden, Peter Finch and Faye Dunaway, tells the story of a television presenter who is about to get fired for his low audience ratings and faced with the tremendous pressure he is under. He decides to transform himself into an anti-establishment preacher, managing to reinvent himself and obtain great media success with a slogan that citizens make their own and shout out every night from their balconies: "I'm as mad as hell, and I'm not gonna take this anymore!" The film is a great satire about the world of television and the big corporations and the establishment itself, showing a more merciless face, hard and unjust, represented by the president of the media corporation, a guy named Jensen, who upon seeing the renewed success of his presenter, invites him to meet one on one, and in the middle of the conversation and faced with the idealist spirit shown by the presenter, Jensen spits out: "Democracy does not exist, the States do not exist, Corporations are the new States."

I cite this brief story to illustrate after more than 50 years, how the world of business has transformed and also in certain ways the values of actual society. If we traverse the world from country to country, we see that no more than a dozen large corporations dominate business and, in some way, the world. I'll explain, names such as Texaco, Aramco, Nestlé, Volkswagen, Bayer, Siemens, Bosch, General Electric, Cisco, Toyota, Samsung, Microsoft, Amazon, Facebook, Apple, etcetera; these are the large corporations and the "new States" to which the character in the film referred. Just remember that Apple in its dispute with the European Union (Brussels) over a question of taxes not properly paid in the states where it earns its revenue, has won the battle against the entire European Union, including a ruling by the supreme tribunal of the European Union. Gives you something to think about, no?

One of the most influential cartels in recent economic history is the Organization of the Petroleum Exporting Countries (OPEC) that was created in 1960 in Baghdad by various producing countries as a response to the dominance by seven multinational companies that had absolute control over the market. Granted, their initial motives were justified and were in some way good for consumers since they promoted competition in the offering of petroleum, we all know what subsequently became of the OPEC. During the next five decades, this organization of producers from various countries in the Gulf, South America and Asia has kept the world economy under its control given the importance of the natural resource they control.

They alone have assumed a true world power within political power, have dictated their prices and their conditions to the whole world and when the conditions were not favorable to them they provoked a major economic and social crisis in the year 1974 when they unilaterally decided to quadruple the price of oil, putting with this decision the entire world economy under horses' hooves. Personally, I still remember it as it was when I had finished my studies, and for me along with many of my classmates it was impossible to find a job as the majority of companies had implemented a hiring freeze in the face of these brutal price increases and rise in costs that caused great uncertainty and a profound recession in the economy.

These corporations are the ones referred to in the film "Network" wherein it affirms that States do not exist and that the large corporations are the new States. However, there is more, apart from petroleum which is the principal raw material that all countries need; we have all heard talk about the steel cartel, the electricity cartel, the food cartel, the pharmaceutical cartel, the automation cartel, the shipping cartel, the tech companies cartel, etcetera, etcetera.

These groups and corporations that hold so much power and that control large sectors and spaces of the economy not only limit themselves to accords amongst them to fix prices, conditions and even rules that affect all citizens, rather in addition they have their own pressure groups, the so called "Lobbies" whose mission is to influence and pressure Governments so that they will legislate in favor of their interests, forgetting the general principle of the economy which is the common good.

We all recall some examples of sanctions imposed by some Governments on certain groups or corporations for their less than ethical and in some cases downright illicit practices. Antitrust Law was implanted in the United States a few decades ago and more recently the EU has also come out with its own anti-monopoly law to put a stop to and occasionally sanction the activities of these groups in certain markets. It is the essence of capitalism that marks the path towards oligopolies.

Every once in a while it appears on the news that a great automotive group has been sanctioned by national or EU regulators; that the practices employed by large corporations for price fixing were not in accordance with the rules for real and transparent competition; that the alliance formed by various food companies had an objective to capture large swathes of the market to distort prices and increase their profits in detriment to consumers; that the large corporations of raw materials have signed an accord to destabilize the markets, creating a false sense of abundance or scarcity, depending on what is most convenient for their interests, that is to speculate, again to obtain greater profits.

Recently we have all seen on television that the Federal Trade Commission of the United States Senate called the four largest tech sector companies to testify, Apple, Amazon, Google and Facebook for certain indications that they were applying certain practices that directly violated Antitrust Law on the fringes of the more or less theatrical representation that was meant by the scheduled appearance, everything ended in some suspicion, some admonishment and light sanctions.

In conclusion, we can see that all of those behaviors and practices of dubious legality provoke a distortion in prices, in competition, and in the markets that make the principle of perfect competition and the self-regulation of the markets propagated by Adam Smith be more wishful thinking by the citizens than a day to day reality.

PRODUCTION AND CONSUMPTION

In traditional societies the primary sector (Agriculture and Fishing) represents 85% or more of activity, the secondary sector (Industry) about 10% and the tertiary sector (Services) about 5%. Notwithstanding, in developed and advanced societies the percentages are inverted in such a manner that the primary sector represents about 5%, the secondary sector about 20% and the tertiary sector represents approximately 75% of a country's production. What does this mean? Well, that as a country develops it goes through one stage or another, going from a subsistence economy to an industrial economy and finally a service economy, such as we have in Spain and in the majority of developed countries.

Today, the most important sector and that which contributes the most value to a country is the service sector, followed by industry and lastly agriculture. In spite of the service sector being the most important in advanced countries, it is, nevertheless, the industrial sector that generates the most jobs and in some way constitutes the spinal column of a prosperous country.

If we take recent data from Spain, Industry represents only 11% of the GDP having reduced this sector in recent years from 25% to the current level. This situation has some direct consequences on the employment level of the country, generating some of the highest unemployment rates in the world, especially among those under the age of 30 where this percentage increases up to 40-50% depending on the regions. If we compare this situation with countries in our surroundings, the industrial sector represents 31% in Germany, 30% in Switzerland, 35% in the Czech Republic, 25% in Italy, etcetera, we observe that these countries not only have a higher quality of life than Spain, but they also have the lowest unemployment rates in the world, between 8-10%. Therefore, it is not difficult to conclude that Spain has a structural deficit in the industrial sector and a job deficit that could be corrected by increasing capital investments and training in industry; Spain needs more industry.

As far as the service sector is concerned, it is also a great job generating secretary, although not as much as industry, and in the specific case of Spain the contribution of value and employment is distorted by the importance of tourism and commerce which depend largely on foreign tourists and that under given circumstances like the current one, reveal an important decline in activity and the receipts in this sector. Additionally, the majority of work contracts are of a high volatility and temporality which means that they do not contribute as they should to adding value and stability to that sector.

It is true that the agricultural sector and agro industries have a relevant importance in this country, representing 15% of the GDP and thousands of jobs. However, here again, the work contracts are in large part temporary and on many occasions they are subject to very precarious situations; with which we may conclude and again I insist… What Spain needs is more industry.

To use just one example, just 30 years ago (1990), China was an underdeveloped country; in the last 20 years China has gone from manufacturing cheap products of little added value to being a leader in Artificial Intelligence (AI), in 5G, electric cars, and battery production. Why has Spain, having better conditions to begin with, fallen so far behind? The answer is that in this country Research, Development and Innovation have never been given the importance they deserve; we all remember that phrase from Unamuno in the past century, "Let them invent". This is one of the greatest scourges that has dragged this country for decades and that in spite of countless studies in existence that have identified the problem, almost nothing has been done.

On the consumption side, we must say that this is logically tied to the income levels available in each country, and to a lesser extent, to consumer habits, although these are more in line with the social class to which one belongs, than to the country where one resides; it is a fact that a homogenization of consumer habits exists in the majority of developed countries, a product of Globalization, of the trends and fashions generated on the Internet.

Many of us remember how in the 1950s and 1960s, mothers were determined to repair, mend and get the most out of dresses, food, toys, books, etcetera, that were handed down from older siblings to younger ones and sometimes even to other family members; the trade economy had not yet become extinct. It was in the 1970s and 1980s when, rooted in immense economic growth, mass consumption and a culture of use and disposal were instilled… which some companies fervently devoted to the capitalist system have known how to exploit with the deliberate installation of built in obsolescence, or to put it another way, with the predetermined life span of thousands of products, after all consumption must continue.

It is an intrinsic condition of the capitalist system that the demand must always come before the offer, it is also an indispensable condition of growth; that is to say, a certain level of inflation (price increases) is always convenient for the system to function correctly, otherwise, meaning, if there is more product than demand or consumption we could enter into a phase of deflation (price decreases) like the current one, which can lead to a reduction in investment, production and jobs in the face of few prospects of profits that business owners may see in the future.

We will not get into assessing consumption habits, since, as we have said, these depend on income levels, distinct cultures, fashion or publicity; we only want to highlight that there has been a radical change in consumer habits in the last 50 years that has provoked some very negative consequences for society and that are reflected in the deterioration of the environment with its grave consequences in climate change which we are seeing, on one hand, and on the other hand, the damaging consequences and the serious problems it is also causing in the health of citizens (obesity, stress, respiratory illnesses, addiction, etcetera) as well as in their living habits, each time getting further away from a frugal and balanced life.

The boom of the sustainable economy and of the collaborative economy are not a coincidence, rather they are a response to an intimate desire of citizens for greater control of their habits and their lives.

Perhaps, one of the few positive consequences that may have resulted from this Coronavirus crisis has been to invite us to briefly suspend our habits and helping us to reflect more carefully on the meaning of our lives, our customs and our consumer habits.

THE CRISES

It is appropriate and pertinent to mention and talk about the crises in a chapter about the economy, although we have already shared that we have devoted an entire chapter in the book to discuss this topic given its importance in the economy and society in general.

As we have already mentioned earlier in this chapter, the majority of economic crises are produced by an increase in runaway inflation or by an exponential rise in the public debt, corporate debt, and consumer debt.

Nevertheless, throughout history there have been great crises that were not a consequence of these factors, rather the causes were outside of the system and of the economy. As a recent example, the actual crisis caused by the Coronavirus.

A quick review throughout human history shows us that there have been great economic crises that had nothing to do with the economy.

These have been caused on various occasions by great climatological catastrophes, illnesses and global pandemics such as the Plague and the Spanish Flu, by civil wars, the possession of other resources or territories, or worse still, by human foolishness and avarice, as happened in the Netherlands in 1637 with the crisis provoked by the Tulip bubble in which the value of half a dozen Tulips reached a higher price than that of a house. The following year, the final Tulip sale did not find a buyer, the prices bottomed out and everyone who had invested in those flowers was ruined and drove the economy of the Netherlands into bankruptcy.

Crises, in spite of the huge disasters and the terrible consequences they provoke, have a positive secondary effect, and that is because after the "drunkenness" there generally comes a state of reflection and meditation that begins to act anew with a more responsible and sensible attitude, behaving as in a state of "do over" that with time manages to regain the previous levels and, on occasion, surpass them.

As we've noted, in one complete chapter to that effect, we will analyze in greater detail the crises, its causes and its consequences.

THE INEQUALITIES

One of the most negative consequences for which the capitalist system has often been criticized is that at the same time as it generates growth and progress, it also creates great inequalities in large swathes of the population; and this is true, although it would have to be qualified in order to be as precise as possible. Capitalism is not a social system of distribution; the essence of the capitalist system is to invest, accumulate and grow capital and profits without taking into account who does it or how they use it; that is what Governments are for, whose primary commitment is to distribute, the distribution and well-being of the population through contribution by way of taxes, of some part of that capital and of those profits.

Bill Aulet, Managing Director of the Martin Trust Center for MIT Entrepreneurship at the Massachusetts Institute of Technology (MIT) says that "there can be no social justice without economic justice". In effect, the wealth and well-being of countries is produced with an important increase in production, with an increase and expansion in commerce or yet, by a technological revolution with the introduction of new machinery and techniques that increase productivity in an important way; this causes an elevation in the accumulation of investment and financing capital that is generally held by the most powerful and best informed classes. Although is also happens in the new economy of knowledge that some individuals who do not belong to those classes and that are particularly well informed and with an entrepreneurial spirit become the protagonists of the boom in new companies, "Start-ups", that with an accelerated growth and based on knowledge they are able to generate new and relevant organizations in the market.

If we briefly review the economic history of the world we see that the social classes have always existed in all societies and of course they continue existing to this day, albeit with fewer differences among them depending on the countries. In ancient Rome there existed the Patriarchs, Plebeians, Slaves, Clients and the Free… later in the Middle Ages there existed basically four social classes: Nobles, Clergy, Artisans and Peasants.

However, from the 18th and 19th centuries everything changed with the first and second industrial revolution during which, after having abolished the bourgeoisie and the nobility with the French Revolution of 1789, there appear and begin to take shape two social classes: the Capitalists and the Working Class.

Those who have capital no longer invest it in more land or real estate as they did previously, instead they now invest in machinery, technology and innovation and all of these investments produce each time more machinery, more technology and more inventions; it is what economics calls an investment multiplier. This has a direct consequence on work and on the creation of thousands of jobs that are progressively occupied by workers, many of them coming from the country and from agriculture.

All of this process that we know as the Industrial Revolution produces and creates more capital each time and also more jobs; with which the different social classes existent in prior centuries are practically reduced into two classes: the minority that holds the capital and the majority of the population who has nothing but its labor force. This new situation, quite unjust for the majority, leads to various revolutions of the proletariat whose main inspiration and ideologue was Karl Marx with his work Das Kapital (Capital: A Critique of Political Economy), but that nevertheless is well less unjust and harsh than what there was in the Middle Age or in Ancient Rome.

We have made this brief review throughout history that will serve to dismantle the argument of the famous phrase "past times were better" and that what is happening today is that the inequalities increase more each time and that poverty is greater each time in wide layers of the population.

During the 20th and 21st century capitalism has produced the greatest expansion of wealth and work to wide sections of the world population; an affirmation that I share as an economist with many other economists of diverse ideologies. It is not only about one affirmation rather it is about a proven empirical evidence. I am not going to give an historical or statistical review to what we have just affirmed, only highlight where and how a great part of the population was at the start of the 20th century and where we are now.

The immense economic, scientific, technological and health progress would have been unthinkable then if we compared both situations of humanity then and now. It is true that the world continues to be divided in two parts; on one side the developed countries that make up the Organization for Economic Cooperation and Development (OECD) and the developing countries that make up the other larger majority part (with the exception of oil producing countries).

That said, it is appropriate to cite the work published years ago by the French economist, Thomas Piketty, "Capitalism in the 21st Century"; a greatly successful book and in certain ways different to what had been published until then on the subject of inequality. The principal thesis proposed by Piketty is that social inequalities will go on growing and will be greater each time, as he affirms that while capital yields (5-10%) grow at a rhythm superior to that of jobs (1-2%), citizens will be poorer each time and inequalities will grow.

The reality, we think, is a bit more complex and diverse than this theory, that does not stop having some truth to it. As an economist and as a citizen who has lived in both developed countries and in developing countries, I would like to make some clarification about this thesis that has had so much success, especially, on the left.

It is true that the capitalist system suffers from a variety of defects as much in its conceptualization as in its practical application, but how do we know, no better system has yet been discovered that can provide the greatest level of wellbeing to citizens which is why we are used to phrases like "it is the least bad of the existing systems", the same as we say about Democracy.

It is equally true that this system in which we live produces in its growth and implementation in many countries some imbalances and inequalities that are in some cases a product of the system, but that in many other cases have nothing to do with it, given that those others are produced by other causes like bad economic policies applied or even generalized corruption (as I myself have been able to prove in some developing country) or even due to an external cause affecting the capitalist system, such as the actual Covid-19 pandemic has been. The pandemic without a doubt will continue to widen these inequalities among diverse sectors given that in the next recovery that is looming in the shape of a K, some sectors like IT will emerge stronger than others such as tourism, leisure, hospitality and aviation which will be the greatest losers; what will without a doubt cause mass layoffs and adjustments that will further widen the differences between the workers in these sectors and the digital economy. I say again, that the thesis of the economist Pinketty appears to me to be poignant and pertinent, but to my judgement, it is partial and incomplete and as such does not adequately reflect the economic reality of societies today.

In a profound and detailed analysis the economist Daron Acemoglu together with James A. Robinson examine and detail in their book "Why Nations Fail", the economies of distinct developed and developing countries, and arrive at the conclusion that countries are neither rich or poor for having a different climate, nor because of their geographical location, nor because of their natural resources, etcetera, they affirm and demonstrate that countries are developed and wealthy or poor and in development primarily due to the good or bad application of economic policies. They give various contrasting examples like North Korea and South Korea in Asia; or Zimbabwe and Sierra Leone in Africa, etcetera.

In conclusion we believe that if capitalism produces great imbalances and inequalities in some countries and in some stages of its development, and even that the technological progress is marginalizing some segments of the population, it is no less true that at least until now it has been the least bad of the systems and the one which has given higher levels of wellbeing to the population.

That is why, as happens in so many other facets of life the best thing would be a "Protected Capitalism"; certainly not in the Chinese style, but definitely a good combination of private initiative, capital and work, together with a regulatory State, administrator and controller of economic laws that govern our societies; perhaps in the Swedish or Finnish style.

TAX HAVENS

In a global market the principal actors, Governments, manufacturers, and consumers should have the same rules; unfortunately, this is not the case. Without fear of being mistaken we may affirm that the States that are legal tax havens and are accepted as such by the rest of the world, constitute the greatest cancer and danger for the world economy.

In effect, according to the IMF the sum total of money that is hidden in these havens and which escapes Fiscal State Authorities is estimated at 8 trillion dollars, that is the equivalent of the GDP of Germany, France and Spain combined. Obviously, the obligatory question for such a lump sum is: Where does all that money come from and how can it arrive in those countries without the Fiscal control of the other States?

The money comes from a fair amount of illegal activities such as the trafficking of arms, drugs, organized crime, human trafficking, money laundering, the black market and government corruption in different parts of the world, etcetera, but it also comes in another important part from "legal" activities like the hiding of corporate profits, financial engineering and speculation.

This huge sum of resources that float around the world with almost no control at all, could eliminate world poverty in one fell swoop; and that is not a gratuitous or political affirmation with leftist leanings. According to the World Bank half of the world population (4.000 M.) lives on less than 5.50 dollars per day; the bank sets the extreme poverty line as those living on less than 3.00 dollars per day; evidently the poverty number in the countries of the OECD has other yardsticks and it is estimated that a state of poverty is reached when one has less than 20.00 dollars a day to live on.

If we make a very conservative calculation, world poverty could be eliminated by dedicating just 10% (1 trillion dollars) of the existing resources in all of the tax havens of the world today.

Of the 8 trillion dollars parked in tax havens, it is estimated that the different States lose 25% in tax revenue (2 trillion dollars) that could be used to improve the general budgets and as a result the wellbeing of the population in each country.

In a very brief overview of the tax havens in existence in the world today there appear not less than 50 States, of which we would have to discount those countries that have traditionally been classified as tax havens, but that due to the international pressure exercised by many Governments and institutions in recent years, they have gone on to form a "lighter" list called countries with low or no taxation (!).

The majority of these tax havens are located outside of the EU and possibly the best known ones can be found in the area of the Caribbean, the USA or in Asia; but to be more exact a dozen or so of these States with very low or lax taxation also exist within the EU as we said in the example given in the first chapter when we talked about Globalization and of the need for Global Regulation, it is not possible that members of the same "league or in the same competition" as is the European Union have "teams" or States like Ireland, the Netherlands, Luxembourg, etcetera, etcetera that do not play by the same rules as the other States. This is not a fair game, constitutes unfair competition and creates imbalances and inequalities in the rest of the States with direct repercussions on their economies and in the general well-being of the population.

CHAPTER FOUR

THE OTHER POLITICS

"Most men who engage in politics are unworthy and it is shameful to associate with them."
(Cicero, Republic, 1,5 century A.D.)

    Politics is the science that deals with the Governance of the State through the art of negotiation to reconcile opposing interests and the establishment of rules that guarantee order and security, with the end of the common good.

In Western culture we can consider the beginning of Democracy, the Government by the people, in ancient Greece, with the constitution of the Assemblies in the "polis" or cities, which were the representatives of the people and were made up of free citizens; the latter may be considered the actual beginnings of Parliaments; keeping a distance, clearly, since actual Parliaments are comprised of the different political parties that represent the people.

In antiquity power was frequently exercised by force, that is to say, by the strongest law. Subsequently, it was the Monarchs and the Governors who ruled in the different territories during various centuries; it wasn't until the French Revolution in 1789 and with the subsequent Universal Declaration of the rights of man that modern democracy arrived and was constituted with the political parties, the Constitution of the United States and thereafter the different European constitutions.

Greece and Rome are the cradles of modern western civilization; it was in those territories where the most relevant political thinkers flourished, like Plato (The Republic), Cicero (Republic), Aristotle, Marcus Aurelus… and their disciples who established the basis of modern political science. Most recently, philosophers and sociologists like Max Weber, Gramsci, and Karl Marx himself have performed an important role in the history of current politics and sociologies in the 19th and 20th centuries. Actually, if we review the majority of western countries we find that the most common form of politics by which they are governed is Democracy.

Nevertheless, if we look more carefully at those same countries, we observe that many of them are no longer governed only by the traditional political parties, conservatives, liberals or leftists, rather in the actual parliaments there is a diversity and sometimes a colorful variety of one series of parties that defend from the most just and actual causes to the most extravagant and radical motives. This takes us to the following analysis of why it has gone from two or three traditional parties to a multitude of parties and in what way they can influence the lives of citizens.

BIPARTISANSHIP - MULTI-PARTISANSHIP

Until the end of the last century there existed a limited number of political parties in the majority of developed countries, between four or five at most, which have governed these States for decades. We are referring to the, so called, traditional political parties such as the conservatives, the leftists, the liberals, the communists and the right wing extremists. If we look at the United States, you have the Republicans and the Democrats; in England, the Tories and Labour; in Germany, the Conservatives (CDU) and the Social Democrats (SPD); in Italy, the Northern League, the Conservatives, the Five Star League; in France, the Republicans, the Democrats, the National Front; in Spain, the Popular Party, the Socialists, the United Left, etcetera. In all of those countries small parties also coexist, but they have scarce parliamentary representation.

If we observe what has happened since the end of the past century and the beginning of the current century, we see how the political landscape has been transformed in the majority of those countries in which the most relevant phenomenon that we may highlight is the birth and expansion of a multitude of political parties of the most diverse beliefs and leanings to the point where in many Parliaments there may be up to 20 or 25 different parties represented, of which the standouts are the Green party, the Ecologist party, the Regionalist party, the Radical party, the New Alternative party, the Vox party, the Libertarian party, etcetera, etcetera.

This new stage does not have to be a bad thing in and of itself given that the confrontation of ideas and diverse political debate tends to be enriching and democratic; the problem arises when all of them want to decide and on occasion make their own proposals valid.

If we ask ourselves what is causing the rise in such numerous new political parties, we may think that it is in response to the new needs of citizens and to the changes that are coming about in society; which is partly true, but only partly, given that if we analyze the true causes of this situation more in depth we believe that, on one hand, it is due to the new generations being fed up with traditional political parties (right, left…) and of their excessively bureaucratic and hierarchical way of functioning. In effect, the new generations have been left very impacted by the excessive cases of corruption aired daily in the press, on television and on social media, as well as the rigidity and the continuous disputes with which these parties function. The young have a more open mentality, more transversal, more functional and flexible about what a political party should be, to the point that if we observe, the majority of new political formations are no longer called the party of… rather the Platform for… the Movement of… Assembly of… etcetera. To the point of spoiling and disparaging the word "Party" in a good part of the electorate, possibly to clearly mark the rejection that many feel towards traditional parties.

On the other hand, the last two crises (2008 and 2010) have impacted the economy with such force and in society, especially where the young are concerned, who have seen how their expectations of having a better life than their parents as it has been going until now, have faded and torn their dreams and their futures to pieces to the point of reaching levels of unemployment in Europe of up to 40% for this section of the population. All of this tied to the good management and expansion of social networks that propagate information almost instantly that young people have, has made them fall into a sort of disenchantment that has favored the birth and spectacular growth, in some cases, of these new political formations as a sign of protest against traditional parties. It has been a way of saying enough! That is where we get the famous phrase, "they no longer represent us".

LEADERS

In "The Republic", Plato said that to govern "the wisest beings must be chosen".

If we review human history from the time of King Solomon up to the leaders who control politics in this day and age we can prove that there have been all sorts: exceptional, outstanding, good, mediocre, bad, cruel, disastrous… History is full of examples that we may classify within these categories; but it is not the purpose of this book to review the best and worst political leaders throughout history. The truth is that these are frequently elected more for their capacity to elicit emotions than for their capacity to lead.

If we only limit ourselves to the past century and the actual one, we can glimpse some of the most relevant and influential biographies of select individuals whose excellent personalities have marked history and the transformation of their countries, generating a great change in their lives. Thinking, for example, of Franklin D. Roosevelt in the United States, Winston Churchill in England, Mikhail Gorbachev in Russia, Konrad Adenauer in Germany, Willy Brandt in Germany, Mahatma Gandhi in India, Mao Tse Tung in China, Olof Palme, Martin Luther King, Salvador Allende, John Paul II and others… all of them, leaders that drove their people to the highest levels of selfesteem, national pride, and social wellbeing.

On the contrary, a different type of more authoritarian and despotic leaders have also occupied a distinguished place in history as is the case of Josef Stalin, V. Ilich Lenin in Russia, Benito Mussolini in Italy, Fidel Castro in Cuba, Adolf Hitler in Germany, Augusto Pinochet in Argentina, Mao Zedong in China, Pol Pot in Cambodia… and others. The majority of these dictators have caused great destruction, misery and oppression in their people and history would prefer to erase them from its memory.

This brief historical review helps us to comment on what political situation many countries find themselves in today, and who their most distinguished leaders are. In this sense, we would like to introduce a personal theory in reference to the method of choosing the country's president nowadays. We all know that in democratic countries the election is made by universal suffrage between the different political parties and that the candidate selected by the winning party with the most votes will be the country's next president. In this respect, we believe it would be convenient to introduce an additional aptitude test, once the candidate of each party has been selected, the same way these tests are conducted during the hiring process in order to fill a position at a company or any institution; specifically, the test we recommend is a personality test that each of the selected candidates must pass, prior to being confirmed as the official candidate of that party for the general elections.

It is possible for this proposal to generate much criticism especially among the most devoted members of each party, but personally, we consider it indispensable, above all when reasonable doubts exist about the special character and the mental state of the candidate aside from his political aptitudes. Can anyone imagine the president of a great corporation, or bank, or even a Ministry of Defense with seriously altered mental faculties? What risks might the associates the clients, or the citizens suffer with a president that bears serious mental disorders? Well then, there is no need for a very sophisticated exercise to see that as much on the right as on the left, in the West or in the East, there have been various leaders whose personalities were not entirely balanced, to put it mildly, instead they suffered from severe psychological mental issues that the world has had to endure and suffer with the disastrous consequences which that has brought. Without going too far and actually we all have in mind some leader of some country who in the present moment is a good reflection of what we have just mentioned. The balanced personality and the mental health of a leader should come before their political qualities since in the end they will be a reflection of the good mental health and level-headedness of the citizens of that country.

GOOD POLITICS

Between the various positives initiated by Luther's Protestant Reformation what stands out is having instilled, via the interpretation of the Bible, a sense of responsibility in men for their actions in the face of God, in front of others and to themselves. I must say that in the Catholic Church and in Catholicism it was not exactly like that; in effect, bad actions could be forgiven by way of confession, and if this was not enough, that is what the famous Indulgences were for which, once paid for at the right price, absolved one of their sins!!

With this, two things were obtained at the same time, on one hand, with this process one was free of their bad actions, on the other hand, the church obtained very advantageous financing for maintaining their excesses and high cost of living, especially among their highest authorities.

The big difference between these two doctrines has had a capital influence between the peoples of the north, generally Protestants and the countries of the south, mostly catholic. Indeed, I lived for eight years between Switzerland, England and France with some time in Germany and I can say that I have been able to prove the aforementioned firsthand. One of the big differences in the practice of politics between the countries of the north and the south, is the sense of responsibility with which they carry out their functions as much in the political class as in civil society, acting and collaborating conjointly for the common good of the citizens; to such a degree that when someone is mistaken or makes an error, the almost immediate response is their resignation from their post. We all remember a certain

English Minister who had to resign his post almost immediately for having claimed the cost of his home gardener as a justified work related expense. Or some German Minister accused of plagiarizing their doctoral thesis who had to give their resignation the following day.

Regrettably and due to the internalized influence of the aforementioned catholic doctrine over centuries, aside from other historical reasons, the countries of the south have been poorly governed for centuries, precisely because of that sense that errors and bad actions are always forgiven in one way or another and are soon forgotten; that is what we are referring to when we talk about the sense of individual responsibility.

This mentality and way of proceeding as much in politics as in the economy and in society is what instigated how, on many occasions, we came to have such bad rulers and social leaders in the countries of the south.

When we have spoken about the good and bad leaders we have referenced some distinguished personalities that have controlled the destiny of those countries at different periods of recent history, like Winston Churchill in England, Charles De Gaulle in France, Chancellor Adenauer and Helmut Kohl or Angela Merkel in Germany, the Prime Minister of Sweden, Olof Palme, Adolfo Suárez in Spain, or Sandro Pertini and Aldo Moro in Italy. All of them have been an example of what we have called "good politics", that is to say, they have been presidents that have sought consensus above all and avoided conflict, they have made difficult decisions at key moments always thinking about the good of their country, they have been open to dialogue and were flexible: they have not allowed themselves to be influenced by currents of radical ideas, nor by groups more or less influential, rather they have acted sensibly and according to their judgement guided before all and in the first place by the reason of the State.

This class of politicians are the ones that best represent what we have given to calling "good politics" which is what makes countries progress and administers the best justice for its citizens.

BAD POLITICS

Bad politics tend to be represented by people who lack their own ideology or whose ideas look more like opportunism of the circumstances or a radical fanaticism or a unique objective as is the taking of power by any means necessary. Here, the end justifies the means.

History is full of examples of bad politics and disastrous politicians. It is clear that the ultimate objective of some leaders or of some political parties is not the common good or anything like it, rather it is to fulfill their ambitions and that of their group with the end of reaching power, or as one Spanish Leftist Leader recently said "The sky is not taken by consensus it must be taken by assault!"

Apart from each person's own ideologies or those of a party, much of the bad derived from bad politics practiced in countries is a product of the little experience and low training level of their leaders.

A valid anecdote would be the presence in the French Assembly at the beginning of the past century of some young assemblymen, who in an effort to convey a certain level of experience and wisdom wore wigs and fake beards to look the part of more experienced people. Plato's phrase in The Republic, cited earlier, "the wisest people must be chosen" is altogether relevant; although wisdom is not learned at a University nor in an accelerated master class; wisdom is acquired through life experience.

I still recall the question that I was asked a few years ago, after leaving a gathering, by an Argentine Doctor friend, living in Spain, the question was: "Listen, since you have lived in South America, why do you believe those countries do not get ahead?" My answer was only two words: "Inefficiency and corruption". I lived and worked for seven years in a Latin American country, with various trips to Columbia and Brazil, so I believe I know the region. I remember on one occasion when I went on a professional visit to a corporate branch in the south of the country and as we passed an industrial zone full of industrial vehicles I was impressed by an especially large one with disproportionate dimensions; I asked my companion who was a native of that area, "What is that immense vehicle? What do they make?" He replied that it was an aluminum company that had been constructed years ago, but was now closed and no longer functioning. The aspect of the exterior surprised me, there were parts of the walls that were oxidized and in a poor state; so I asked another question, "Why was it constructed?" My companion, without batting an eyelash, replied that it had only been constructed to hand out good commissions between the minister on duty and some assessors!

As we have already noted, in all of the world there are good governments and bad, efficient leaders and disastrous ones. To my understanding, one of the main reasons why some developing countries do not improve is due to the low professional and personal quality of their leaders and because of the extended corruption at all levels of the administration. We could also add a misguided political ideology generally attributed to the extreme left that has already provided abundant proof of its inefficiency throughout history.

Many countries on a development track appear to have not understood that politics is not only a question of ideology but primarily a matter of good organization and efficient management.

Regrettably, the leaders of several of those countries have reached power via Coups d'Etats or by other not so democratic means. In these circumstances, justice, private property and the common good, become words devoid of content and many of those countries are dragged and kept in a desperate situation from which it is very difficult to emerge. That is "bad politics".

POPULISM

The distinct economic and social crises experienced throughout the course of history are the best breeding ground for the birth of populist leaders. History is full of examples; the causes of these populisms are relatively easy to explain. In the majority of cases it is about taking advantage and manipulating the "desperation of the people" in exceptional circumstances, to gain power.

The term "Populism" means politics by and for the people, its objective is to grow closer to the people and better understand their needs and hopes with an end of providing a solution in the most just manner possible and when this is not possible by peaceful means, then employ revolt and revolution to meet their objective. Populist leaders are characterized by making believe that they are the ones that best "understand" their people and the ones that best represent their desires. The most relevant examples of populist leaders in ancient Athens and Rome were Pericles and Julius Cesar; the first, dictated a series of decrees that reduced the privileges of the upper political class to give them to the people and in the case of Julius Cesar his power came from the people since with his great sensibility he got the Roman Senate to distribute land among the most poor, as well as the recognition of certain rights that the popular classes did not previously have. It could be said that these leaders were "good populists".

However, it has not always been so; more recently, Populism has frequently had a pejorative connotation given that it is almost always associated with demagogue leaders who deceive the people. In fact, the origin of populism goes back to ancient Greece where there was proliferation of demagogues (demos: people; gogos: guide/lead) who possessed a great oratory ability and by employing sophisms and other trickery attempted to convince the people to join their causes or gain their objectives, which in the end were all the same, that is, gaining power and great privileges with the excuse of favoring the people.

In the past century and during the first part of this one, a series of populist leaders have proliferated in different regions of the world that, although they are generally almost always associated with the political current of the leftists, we have had theme from both sides, that is to say, as much from the left as from the right. Actual populism comes from the last century with the approach of the privileged elites in Russia when attempting to take an interest in the people given the terrible economic and social conditions suffered by the peasants and the working class; deep down, this was the origin of the subsequent communist revolution that fed up with suffering the consequences of the immense privileges enjoyed by the royal family of the Czars and their entire circle as well as certain intellectual elites, this situation gave way to the Bolshevik Revolution of 1917 with the taking of the Winter Palace and the exile and subsequent assassination of the Czar and his family.

In the middle of the past century the Peronist dictatorship was established with the arrival in power of Juan Domingo Perón; possibly one of the most significant leaders of what we call Populism. The reasons for Perón's arrival at power are similar to those that have happened in other countries: that is to say, the people's frustration and the feeling of having had enough with the dire living conditions they endured as a consequence of corruption and inefficiency of their leaders. Populisms have never gotten along well with the intellectual elites; in fact, at that time in Argentina there existed a relevant intellectual class formed by philosophers, and writers who immediately revealed themselves as anti-Perón, but without much success. Perón repealed and dictated a series of reformative laws that especially favored the people, nevertheless his slightly dictatorial methods made it so that after nine years he had to resign.

We could find other populist leaders in America and Europe in the second part of the last century and even now. The common denominator we always find is a crisis and a great discontent among the people; that is why populist leaders are also called "Homeland Saviors". What can you say about a modern populist like the president of the United States with his "America First" or "Make America Great Again"? Also, the president of Brazil with his slogan "Brazil above all and God above all", or the Italian politician Mateo Salvini, "Italians first, then immigrants", or in South America with Hugo Chavez and his successor Nicolás Maduro; or in Italy with Silvio Berlusconi with his "Forza Italia" political party, or Marine Le Pen in France with her anti immigrant rhetoric…etcetera…or in North Korea and Thailand were dictators rule.

The essential argument in populist discourse is the call to nationalism, it is the exaltation of the nationalist sentiment and of the word Nation in wide swathes of the population, generally the most disadvantaged, given that populism must always find an enemy "real or fictitious" to sustain its discourse and encourage the masses. In this sense, the potential enemies of the nation could be anything from the immigrants, to the successive economic crises, or the privileged political and social elites, or even technology… each one of them represents a danger to the country and its citizens and as such they must be firmly combatted, appealing to the deepest feelings and most respected values of citizens with the goal of motivating and joining them to the cause of the populist leader. The end is clear, it is the taking of power.

We could ask ourselves why in these latest times so many populist leaders have surged in diverse regions of the world. To our judgement this phenomenon has a lot to do with the numerous changes that are happening in society at all levels, especially in technological innovation and in the gradual increase to the inequalities among countries and among the different sectors of society. As we said at the beginning, human beings need certain truths and securities to survive and make sense of their life; and such an accelerated and disruptive change as is happening, above all in this century, makes the citizen look for an anchor point by which to hold their self up and continue believing in their self and in the institutions, for that they are willing to buy the discourse of those leaders that know how to better understand and guide them.

We believe that the promotion of education and culture on the part of governments together with the eradication of poverty are the best antidotes for developing free citizens with solid foundations to prevent the populist phenomenon from continuing to repeat itself in the future.

LEFTS - RIGHTS

In August of 1789 after the start of the French Revolution the question of the Royal Vote was put to a vote in the French Assembly, that is to say, whether the King could vet some resolution taken by the Assembly and when voting they were divided into two camps, on the right side of the President were seated the nobility and the clergy and on the left side were the representatives of the common people and the small bourgeoisie. This little anecdote was the beginning of what we now call the left and the right and whose term extended rapidly throughout Europe and later the rest of the world.

In the beginning, the so-called right defended values such as economic freedom, private prosperity, order, religion, authority, tradition, and legal security. On the contrary, the left defended values like progress, solidarity, equality, secularism, and social justice. If we notice today, the significance that those two terms have, we can see how they have changed and evolved.

When we talk about the right we generally refer to an ideological current or a political position that primarily defends, economic freedom, the individual against the State, private initiative, private prosperity, private property, progress by way of work and merit, and religious values.

The left may be defined today by the State's defense of well-being, the common good, equality among individuals, the defense of the State over the citizen, progress also called progressivism, etcetera. Definitely, the Left gives more importance to the State as the principal agent of progress and social justice, whereas the Right essentially values the individual and their private liberty as an engine and agent of progress in society. They are then two distinct views of politics, of the role of the State and of the role of the individual in society.

The principal social movements born after the French Revolution of 1789 sought to change the social order in force until then constituted primarily by the King, the aristocrats and the bourgeoisie as dominant powers with the end of constituting a more egalitarian society.

That is when divergent political currents were born well into the 19th century, and whose greatest exponent was the Communist Manifesto of 1848 and subsequently the publication of "Das Kapital" in 1869 by Karl Marx together with Engels and whose primary thesis was the "the struggle of classes" that would later inspire so many Anarchist movements, Trotskyism, communism, socialism, and finally social democracy.

This not being a book, not even a chapter dedicated to the analysis of the different currents and political ideologies throughout history. The mission and the end of this aside within a brief analysis of the actual predominant political tendencies is to clarify and shed some light on what the majority of people understand, what the political rights and the lefts stand for and in what way they may have influence on society and on their lives.

On the other hand, it would be a bit pretentious on our part to delve into an in depth and historical analysis of these thought currents that have meant so much for humanity.

If we accept the fact that the two most significant political currents today continue to be the Right and the Left, or the liberals and the socialists; without forgetting other parties, as we have already mentioned, no less relevant like the ecologist party, the nationalist party, and the different regionalist parties, we observe a certain regression of many of these parties that act with a certain regressive parallelism as when we spoke about Globalization and Deglobalization.

This political and economic regression follows, in our judgement, two factors primarily: on one side, the citizens of certain regions want to defend their own identity and their nationalist values in the face of what they consider a loss of control and specific autonomy, brought on by Globalization and its standard values; and on the other, they want to take back control of their politics and their decisions that they consider usurped in recent times by the birth of supranationalist entities like the EU or institutions like the IMF or the OECD; that have lost the content and purpose of their national identity. There we have the examples of Catalonia, Hungary, Poland, Wales and Scotland or the North League and Padania in Italy.

The objectives of the left and of the right are basically the same: the Safeguarding of the State, the common good, justice, and the wellbeing of citizens; these two political currents differ only in their methods and the road to reach them. It is there where the phenomenon of change comes in full and how this may affect the lives of citizens depending on the prevalence of the application of one system or another in the different countries.

From experience and from having lived in countries with right wing politics and also in countries with left wing politics I must say that I have followed some cases and in other cases I have put up with the consequences derived from the application of one ideology or another, and I have seen and proven over the terrain the positive results in some countries and the disastrous consequences in others. These personal experiences have led me to ask myself, why, in general, Anglo-Saxon countries obtain better economic and social results in the application of their politics than many countries in the south of Europe and Latin America?

It is true that the point of departure among them is of a different point of entry, which would be explained by a certain advantage of Anglo-Saxon countries as far as culture, knowledge, technology, and a protestant morale are concerned. But although this would explain part of this advantage, what would explain the other part, that is to say, why certain southern countries, in general, obtain worse results in the application of their leftist politics, would be, we believe, by an inefficiency and a generalized corruption at entrusting a large part of leftist politics to some Governments with little experience in the management and planning of their economies and which are also extremely politicized. The examples are there, in countries like Venezuela, Cuba, Bolivia, Nicaragua and even closer in some Eastern Bloc countries like Russia and Belarus or in Asian countries like North Korea or Vietnam…

When we talk about the new politics that have been instituted in the majority of modern democracies we are referring to that substantial change that there has been in the majority of parliaments and that has changed the two tone color, left, right, of these for decades to become one of the new multicolored and multi partisan institutions where some parties, no matter how small, have enough with two or three representatives to have a decisive influence in certain moments that may lead to a change in the decisions and the direction of Governments and the political life of a country.

THE WEIGHT OF THE STATE

The state apparatus in the various countries is determined primarily by its political regime; there are "thicker" States and "lighter" States according to the level of centralization or decentralization they have and also according to their political affiliation; with the regimes of the left being heavier in general than those of the right. A North American President already said it, the State must be as small as possible and at the same time as efficient as possible (Ronald Regan).

In the case of Spain we are clearly on the heavier side; you only have to look at the number of ministries, 23, that this government has compared to the 16 of South Korea, which is a country similar to ours in terms of population, or the 16 ministries of Germany, which has almost twice the population of Spain, or the 19 of France, which has 12 million more inhabitants than Spain.

According to Eurostat, in Spain there are about 3.1 million public employees, a figure that is in the European average in terms of the number of employees but in terms of total expenditure it represents 15.5% of the country's total employment compared with 11% in Germany with twice the population. As if that were not enough, we have some 400,000 political employees in Spain collecting state salaries compared to 150,000 in Germany. These are employed in all different kinds of public bodies, semi-public companies, observatories of various types, various agencies, municipalities, councils, etcetera, etcetera.

For the first time this year, the salaries paid by the State have surpassed the salaries paid by the private sector by half a million (500,000 more salaries). Specifically, in January 2020, people dependent on the State or the public sector amounted to 8.9 million pensioners, 3.2 million public employees and 1.9 million recipients of various types of aid; in total, 14 million people collect a public salary, compared to 13.5 million in salaries paid by the private sector (this is excluding the 3 million freelancers) according to the EPA from January of this year.

The most efficient States are those that have a more reduced Government and public sector; look at Ireland, Holland, Germany, Switzerland… The problem of countries with large Governments and excessive public employees is that in some fashion many of those jobs have been custom-made to satisfy the parties and the political class that votes for them. In reality, they are political tolls that the Governments in place must pay to keep their base satisfied and have a number of votes secured to insure the next elections.

If we compare the salaries, supplements and other perks that politicians and many of the public employees have against the salaries in the private sector, the latter is also harmed and it is understood that it is difficult to have a light and efficient State this way.

The average gross remuneration of an official in 2019 was 2,654.40 euros per month compared to 1,772 euros of average salary in the private sector; that is, a public employee earns on average 50% (882 euros) more per month than an employee in the private sector (source INE 2019).

Recently, in September 2020, Italy set an example of coherence and austerity in keeping with the times for the majority of citizens who see their jobs at risk, so that the government has approved a reduction of 40% of its Representatives and Senators and the sum of both chambers will be reduced from 945 to 600 with which the State will save 100 million euros a year. Why is a similar measure not approved in Spain? Why can a representative retire at age 60 in Spain and claim a retirement with only 10 years of service, when other citizens are required to work 40 years and retire at age 67? Something important has to change in this country if we want to continue maintaining the state of wellbeing and social peace.

CHAPTER FIVE

DEMOGRAPHY

"Demography is not a safe destination, but it is a significant determinant of economic potential."

Within eighty (80) years, in the year 2100 Spain will have half of the population it currently has, that is 24 million inhabitants, according to the predictions of the Institute for Health Metrics and Evaluation of Washington recently published in the prestigious journal, The Lancet. In previous studies carried out by the UN the projections of the increase in population towards the end of the century were estimated at some 10 billion people in the entire world which made the predictions of the impact on food, health systems, and the environment quite somber. Nevertheless, in various studies after 2017 among which the one previously mentioned in The Lancet stands out, these predictions counter with tighter calculations and forecast that the world population will continue to grow until 2065 when it will reach 9.5 billion inhabitants, but that from then on a decline will begin and the year 2100 will be reached with a population of no more than 8.8 billion inhabitants on earth.

These more "optimistic" predictions for the lesser impact on the environment and on natural resources, would be primarily due to two factors: first, to an important decline in birth rates especially in Europe and Asia, and second, by the mass use of contraceptive methods in the majority of the population. Evidently, the impact would not be the same in all regions; for example, many countries in Europe and Asia would see their population reduced nearly by half as in the case of Spain, Italy, Portugal and Poland in Europe and by 25% in China, India, South Korea and Thailand in Asia… and likewise for up to 35 countries. On the contrary, in Africa the population would increase, highlighting the case of Nigeria which would surpass the 90 million current inhabitants to more than 450 million by the end of the century. It must be taken into account that these projections may become significantly altered by migratory movements.

What is certain is that the population of people over the age of 65 years old will increase in a considerable way until it reaches 2.7 billion, always according to these estimates, especially in the most developed countries, which would propose some important changes in the social and labor areas and would force the majority of governments to reassess their economic politics and geopolitics for the future, since the centers of power and decision will have changed significantly by then.

The two most realistic solutions proposed by the cited study to avoid population decline and the loss of power and influence in those countries, is that their Governments promote active family planning policies to increase the number of wanted children and at the same time adopt a more liberal policy with regard to immigration, softening the control measures.

At the sight of this landscape, not at all optimistic for the majority of countries and the world in general, we can make some reflections for as Peter Drucker says in his book "Management Challenges for the

21st Century", "The demographic problem is not only a question of statistics or estimates", according to him, among the five most important certainties that will happen in the 21st century, "the sinking of the birthrate in the developed world" will probably be the most relevant and that which will have the greatest consequences as much at the economic level as at the social and also political level. I continue citing the author when he says that, "during the next twenty or thirty years, demographics will dominate politics and it will inevitably be politics of enormous turbulence". No country is prepared for the conflicts… and continues to ask itself: is delaying the retirement age a thing of the right or the left?... is encouraging people of age to continue working after 60 by giving them tax exemptions on a portion of their income progressive or conservative?

"Equally conflictive for the politics in many countries, will be the challenge of mass immigration, given that at the same time as population decreases in developed countries, it increases in third world countries; and attempting to impede this phenomenon is like impeding the law of gravity." (end quote)

The birth rates in the majority of developed countries sit between 1 and 1.5 children per woman, totally insufficient not only for population growth, but not even enough to assure generational replacement or maintaining the same population level, for which a minimum birth rate of 2.1 children per woman is needed. In the case of Spain, specifically, we are at a birth rate of 1.23 children per woman and there are countries that are even below that.

It is said that the great catastrophes like war, a pandemic, a great hurricane, etcetera, tend to bring a notable increase in population in their aftermath with an increase in births; but it has been proven that this is not the case, at least nowadays; a given example is the great New York blackout of 1965 and it was said that the following year there was an explosion in births, this was also not the case. Unfortunately, after such devastating events, there tends to be a reduction in births and in the population during the following two or three years, such as occurred after the Great War, or the Spanish flu, or from the last financial crisis, or as will be seen following the Covid-19 pandemic.

Just as it happens in other areas of life, after these catastrophes people become more cautious, more skeptical of the future, and more frugal in anticipation of what may come; with which planning to have more children tends to get postponed. Besides, today we have family planning methods that did not exist in the past. On the other hand, the higher economic and cultural level attained in developed countries paradoxically supposes a halt in the increase of new births, which corroborates the low reproductive rates we mentioned earlier.

The demographic phenomenon that assumes the population collapse in wide regions of the world has more to do with a notorious change in culture and the system of values in modern societies rather than with purely economic matters. This change that is coming about in world demographics will at the same time cause radical changes in the areas of work, health, leisure, social relations and politics. We are already living this, and we will see it with more clarity in the next ten, twenty, or thirty years.

At some moment of our lives we will all suffer from one or several bouts of flu with the well-known consequences of a headache, fever, congestion, body aches, respiratory difficulties, etcetera. In 1918 one of the deadliest epidemics in history occurred, the poorly named, Spanish Flu, which in reality originated in the United States of America in parallel with Asia and was apparently brought to Spain by some American soldiers stationed in our country… in that year, the world population hovered around 1.820 billion inhabitants and because of the cited flu 50 million people died, especially the young. This flu, apparently, was very much linked to the unsanitary conditions caused by World War I. This episode caused a 2.5% drop in the world population in just a couple of months, in actuality thanks to the flu vaccines, only around 500,000 people die each year in the entire world. Fortunately, nowadays we are better prepared and in the face of the actual Coronavirus pandemic, it is expected that with the introduction of vaccines in a few months, the impact on the population will be 200 times less than it was back then, taking into account the actual population of 7.5 billion.

This historic episode serves us to illustrate that aside from the great humanitarian catastrophes that have occurred in the past and have in part diminished the population, what we can affirm is that the increase in world population between the beginning of the 20th century (1.8 billion) and the 21st century (7.5 billion) has been spectacular and unique in the history of humanity; until then the population doubled every several centuries; and today, in only one century, the population has multiplied by four; this has been possible primarily for two reasons: the spectacular progress of medicine and medical care, and the improvement in nutrition and in the living conditions of the population, that has caused a radical decline in the infant mortality rate, and an increase in people's life expectancy.

The demographic transition (deaths / births) shows in the last half century that in developed countries the number of births is lower each time and the number of deaths and the amount of people over the age of 65 increases; on the contrary, in developing countries, primarily in Africa, the tendency is reversed, that is to say, each time there are more births and more young people of working age and each time there are more deaths and fewer elderly people.

As a result of this quite disparate evolution between both parts of the world, the form of the population pyramid in wealthy nations resembles more and more the shape of a mushroom, wide at the top (many elderly people) and narrow at the bottom (few young people);

meanwhile in poor nations it continues to hold the shape of a pyramid, that is, wide at the bottom (more young people) and narrow at the top (few elderly people).

The consequences of all of these movements in the world population will bring about important changes in many countries that will see themselves seriously affected in their structures, in their job markets, housing, health systems, education system, their immigration policies, social assistance programs, and in their geopolitical position in the world.

To this end, governments should have in mind a mid-range and long-term plan and forecasts on the most appropriate management of the demographic issue and its future development in their countries.

The first country that seems to have understood this issue is China, which with its 1.3 billion inhabitants wants to be the world's leading power and it seems that it will soon succeed; it is already the second economic power after the United States and will make good the phrase with which this chapter begins, that demography is not a safe destination but it is a determinant of economic potential; confirming at the same time that quote from Max Weber which says "For its development, capitalism requires the existence of an excess of population which it may rent out at low prices in the labor market".

THE JUNIORS

The Millennial generation, that is to say, those born at the end of the 1980s and beginning of the 1990s is probably the generation that will have known two great economic Depressions before reaching the age of thirty, meanwhile many of them have not yet incorporated themselves into the labor market. This new situation will mean that the vision of the new generations of the world in general, of work, of politics, and of leisure will have very little to do with the vision and tastes that their parents had at the same age.

If we accept that good training, whether vocational or at a university, is of paramount importance for young people in order to develop and be able to undertake a vital project for the future, the fact is that this often depends on the country in which they reside. For example, the youth unemployment rate in countries such as Spain or Italy or Greece is around 35%, while in countries such as Germany, Austria or Denmark it is less than 8%. This is largely due to the different training system in place in some countries or others. The low level of youth unemployment in the latter countries is mainly due to what is called dual training; which basically consists of a three- or four-year period during which a youth is trained both at school (30%) and at a company (70%) with that work study relationship. This system provides both young people and businesses with a real opportunity to acquire real training and experience in the world of work that could hardly be acquired in school alone, such that once that stage is complete, the majority of youth find work in the same company that has trained them; and at the same time, those companies count on workers that are fully functioning from day one after finishing that cycle.

The two most important factors for youth to undertake a project of a relatively stable and independent life are: have a job and as such a steady income, and adequate housing in accordance with their personal circumstances. These are the two indispensable requirements so that any country may configure a stable population of working age and which serves as a means and impetus to the growth of that country's GDP. If this is not the case, protest movements and the transfer of population from one country to another that offer better opportunities to carry out the life project that we talked about begin to develop. This phenomenon which we call emigration or immigration has some direct and almost immediate consequences both in the countries of origin as in the countries receiving that population, with the receiving countries generally benefitting from immigrants; given that these are generally young people of working age and as such will come to reinforce and augment the production and population of the country.

Having a stable job today and a salary is becoming almost a privilege in many places for many young people and sometimes also for those who are past the age of 50. The accelerated changes that are taking place in various areas such as markets, technology, trends, fashions etc … they only confirm this fact. Having a job and a salary means being able to consume, to be able to save and invest and also pay taxes; these three activities derived from having a salary determine good economic health of the worker and of the economy of the country.

As we have commented, the two primary factors that determine the increase in the population of a country are: the increase of the birth rate coupled with an open immigration policy, and on the other hand, the existence of both employment and housing opportunities to make that population stable and settled in the territory.

In this regard, in the case of Spain, the latest statistics show that the evolution of housing prices in recent years has risen at double the rate of workers' salaries. In this way, if twenty years ago 3 annual salaries were needed to buy a home, today it would take on average between 6 and 7 annual salaries to purchase a home. This makes it increasingly difficult for couples to settle in a specific place, and at the same time makes it difficult to plan to have more children, precisely because of high housing prices along with the increasingly insecure possibility of having a stable job. That is why, as long as young people under the age of 35 do not see or perceive the possibilities and more opportunities for work and housing in the country in which they live, an increase in the population of young people, which is the desired objective of most governments, since this increase has a direct impact on the rise in GDP, will not happen, unless this increase comes from the immigration side.

On the other hand, the low wages and precarious contracts that most of these young people receive will generate two pernicious effects on society: on the one hand it will cause the population to decline since many of them will seek opportunities in another country, and on the other hand, the maintenance of the pension system will become increasingly difficult because while the population over 65 years of age is the one that increases, the population and the wages of the youngest are the most diminished, which means the system will become more and more unsustainable each time as a result of this difference, given that it is the youth that support the pensions of the elderly in a system of distribution such as the one we have.

While today, most young people can enjoy many cheaper consumer goods than those that were accessible to their parents such as the Internet, video games, travel, leisure … the main assets for any family such as housing, education and work have become almost inaccessible. We therefore believe that the governments of many countries should take this situation of young people into account, as they are the future of the country, in order to alleviate their increasing frustration and give them more hope in their future thereby avoiding the growing protests and revolts that have already been seen in recent times in various countries.

THE SENIORS

At the start of the 20th Century the life expectancy in developed countries was 45 years; today in 2020, this number is situated at 80 years and increases continuously. In one century the life expectancy has doubled. I think we must consider this phenomenon as a great triumph of humanity and science. Paradoxically, in antiquity and epochs prior to the 21st century elders have always been held in high regard, save exceptions, for their experience, wisdom, and empathy for understanding and guiding the youngsters. There are examples of Japan, South Korea, and even China where punishments and sanctions exist for youth that do not respect or care for their elders.

Nowadays, however, it is irritating and almost shameful to witness the little respect and the lack of admiration that our elders elicit among the new generations of youth, in the west, imbued by a culture of youth worship as a supreme value, by some values of the here and now, and by a technology that inundates it all and which has transformed and not exactly in a positive way, human relations.

Any statistic that we choose shows us that the age group that is growing the most in the majority of western countries and in Asia is that of people over the age of 65 years old, the collective that is growing the most, well above the very young, of 0-5 years and youth of 5-15 years, in such a way that the group of people older than 65 years which today represents between 15-20% of the population in developed countries, will go on to represent 30% of the population in 2050, and 40% in 2100 at the end of this century with a total of 2.7 billion which will mean that 1 out of every 3 people within 30 years will be a Senior Citizen.

Faced with this new scenario of the distribution of the population in the world, it is worth asking what role our elders will play in the new society of the coming decades. We can infer without a doubt that the position that seniors will occupy in the near future will be a relevant and positive role both for the economy, for young people and for society as a whole. We believe that an intelligent and progressive society in the future cannot squander and do without the experience, wisdom, and human values of older people. It is too valuable an asset for society and for future governments not to take it into account.

Ever since Cicero, year I a.c., wrote his eulogy of old age in "De Senectute" where he describes the benefits and good sides of being older, as long as there is reasonable physical and economic health, history is full of examples of elderly people who have practiced their profession and sometimes given their best of themselves at very advanced ages. A few cases in point, in Venice the doges (magistrates) who ran the city were of average age 70 years, people like Victor Hugo in France was elected a representative at the age of 75, Verdi composed the Traviata, one of his best works at 75; Michelangelo finished painting the dome of St. Peter in Rome at 80; more recently Pablo Picasso was still painting in his 90s; Pau Casals was once asked by a journalist why he was still rehearsing in his 90s and he replied to keep improving…

At present and with the prospect of an increase in life expectancy experienced in recent decades and for the future, it is necessary to assume that more and more people will be over the official retirement age of 65 or 70, will remain active and will be able to continue offering benefits and value to society.

As we discussed at the beginning of this chapter, the length of life and the increase in the population group over 65 years of age will bring a series of changes and consequences in several stages of society. Every day we will see in the workplace and in companies more generational diversity where a young person of 30 years works together with one of 70 years; in gyms every day it is more frequent to find people of 35 or 40 years next to gentlemen of 75 practicing their preferred activity; it is frequently seen in parks, on the street or in marathons, young people of 25 running alongside 80 year old men… in the end, as Mark Twain said, "Age is a question of mind over matter, if you don't mind, then it does not matter".

The important repercussions that this change and increase in life expectancy is already having on society and on the economy of many countries may be observed in the increase and change in the consumer habits of the elderly; thus, for example, we can see the exponential growth of private health insurance companies whose main customers are those over 65 years of age; the increasing number of clients of travel agencies and tour operators; the growth of patients in hospitals and private clinics of anti-aging treatments and personal care; the increase in the number of careers for older people; the rise in demand for and consumption of "bio" food and products; the growth in residences for the elderly; the increase in self-employed and business registrations recorded in recent years in people over 65 years of age. All these new activities that previously hardly existed, have been driven and produced by many people who have long since exceeded the legal retirement age, bringing with them an increase in the economic and social activity of a country and hence its wealth.

"In Praise of Slow" is a book published in 2019 and written by Scottish journalist Carl Honoré in which he reviews the benefits of becoming older and also talks about the less pleasant things, although the overall balance is clearly positive. There is a current of thought in our society called "Ageism", which is not limited only to what young people think of their elders, there are also other swathes of the population that in some way are also impregnated with that mentality.

Ageism is a pattern of thinking that believes every person over the age of 65 years is an old person and therefore does not count for much in society; they are considered depreciated, slow, behind the times and clumsy in the digital age, etcetera, etcetera. We believe that the days are numbered for this way of looking at older people. In everyday life it is becoming more notable and palpable to see people of 60, 70 or 80 years old leading a completely normal and active life as if they were people of 30, 40 or 50 years old… as the Portuguese Neurobiologist, Antonio Damasio once said, "the sixties are the new forties".

We all have in our family circle or among our friends, people who have long since reached the age of 65 and who are still active and developing the most diverse activities, some dedicating themselves to their favorite hobbies, others starting a professional reinvention because they see that they still have a future, many attending courses of various kinds, some, even starting a new economic activity, or taking charge of a charitable institution or some other association for social pursuits. The majority playing sports regularly and planning their next trip or cruise.

But without wanting to give a distorted and somewhat idyllic image of the so-called 3rd age, the great change that has occurred in this segment of the population that only a few years ago practically sidelined from active society is no less true, and today they constitute a social and economic force that dynamically drives the growth of GDP with its demand, their consumption, and their increasingly important activities, in most countries. It is estimated that by 2030 one out of every three jobs will be created for this age group. Governments will have to take this segment of the population more into account, although they should be dedicating more resources to attend to the needs of this group in healthcare, pensions and social assistance.

TRENDS

By 2050 the world's population will have reached 9.6 billion people; 2 billion more than at present according to UN estimates. This increase will come mainly from the countries of Africa and Asia where birth rates are particularly high, 46 births per 1000 inhabitants, while in Europe it barely reaches 8 births per 1000 inhabitants. In the meantime the highest mortality rate is found in eastern European countries (15 per 1000 inhabitants) and in some African countries.

On the other hand, it will also be necessary to take into account the migratory movements that, for various reasons, economic, political, health or education, have mobilized between the different countries in recent decades until 2019 about 70 million people among which there are 26 million refugees. At the same time, currently 55% of the world's population lives in urban environments and by 2050 it is estimated that up to 70% of the population will live primarily in cities.

According to projections of the United Nations (UN), one out of every three people will be over the age of 65 by 2050 and in the next decade, the increase in this age group will be 46%; at the same time the increase in people older than 80 years will surpass the 143 million in 2019 to 426 million by 2050.

Thus, we are headed toward an increasingly aged world, at least in developed countries like the United States and Europe. The counterweight will be placed by Africa where population growth in some countries like Nigeria will more than triple along with an Asian country like India or Indonesia and a Latin American country.

If we focus on the countries of the northern hemisphere, it has been said in various forums, by some politicians, that we will emerge reinforced, stronger and even better from the current Covid-19 pandemic; let me tell you that I do not agree very much with that assessment; I think we will come out being worse physically and mentally, and above all we will be fewer (there are already millions of deaths from the pandemic).

According to UN statistics, the world's population is ageing. If in 1970 the average age of the population was 21.5 years, today in 2020 it is 31 years. By continent, the oldest is Europe with an average of 42.5 years, while the average age in Africa is 19.7 years. On the other hand, the lowest life expectancy is concentrated in some African countries such as Lesotho, Sierra Leone, Central African Republic...

meanwhile, countries with the highest life expectancy are Switzerland, Japan and Spain, in that order.

By continent, in 1900 25% of the world's population was concentrated in Europe; by 2050 it will have only 7% of the world's population. The consequences of this development could be dramatic because we could find ourselves with a European continent saturated with elderly people whose sustenance would represent an enormous challenge and an administrative burden for many of the States whose social protection systems would be seriously compromised.

The causes for the low birth rates indicated in most developed countries are diverse, but there are three that, to our judgment, stand out, such as: the recent economic crises; the fear that these circumstances have generated in families about wanting to increase the number of children, and on the other hand, immigration that in its day was a source of the increase in the population, increasingly immigrant mothers join this wave of family restriction influenced by the restrained behavior they observe in the mothers of their adopted countries.

All of these movements and behaviors are producing in some regions what some sociologists have called "the empty generations", that is to say, the fact that fewer and fewer children are born in developed countries has to do, not only with a somewhat selfish imitation effect, or by essentially individualistic values where what prevails is the individual over the tribe as it was in the past in traditional societies, but the problem is that with such a marked drop in birth rates, in a few years, it turns out that there will not be enough mothers and fathers of reproductive age and therefore this will cause the interruption of the demographic current.

The consequences of these circumstances and events in recent decades suggest that by 2050 some 23 countries in Europe and Asia will have half the population they currently have, as described by Canadian demographers Darrel Bricker and John Ibbitson in their latest book "The Empty Planet". This contrasts with the more alarmist forecasts about the trend towards overpopulation in the world that some leading authors have predicted in the past.

CHAPTER SIX

THE CRISES

"In moments of crisis only the imagination is more important than knowledge."
(Albert Einstein)

Throughout history there have been different crises that have shaped and sometimes radically transformed the systems, values, thought, and order in force in the societies of the time. When we talk about crisis we refer to a time or a stage in history in which "the old does not entirely die and the new does not finish being born" as Einstein himself says. It is usually a period where multiple changes converge and take place in the way of living, in beliefs, in the means of production, in the way of having fun and even in the subversion of the established order when a new technological revolution or political ideas arise. Crises and change always go hand in hand and we must not forget that the economy moves in cycles.

If we review the different crises there have been in history, we see that they are not all alike, they do not have the same causes, nor do they produce the same consequences… One of the first crises originated in the 14th century (1348) as a consequence of the black plague which reduced the population of the European continent of the period by half; this one also saw itself aggravated by the different wars sustained by feudal lords, coupled by a few years of poor harvests which generated some great famines in the population.

With this we wish to say that the causes of the crisis are sometimes produced by a single event and at other times by the confluence of various factors that happen at the same time and place or sometimes in far off places such as now, generally producing disastrous consequences for the countries and their populations.

As we say, crises and financial bubbles have been repeated in a more or less cyclical way since the Middle Ages, even since the Roman Empire whose decline originated in large part by the immense debt accumulated to support the numerous armies it maintained in various territories. More recently, the tulip crisis of 1637 in Holland was one of the first dated bubbles that originated from the exponential rise in the price of tulips to such an extent that on the Amsterdam stock exchange, one tulip came to cost more than a house.

All of the financial bubbles that have ended up turning into financial crises have repeated the same pattern of behavior: an asset begins to rise in price prompted by the idea that it will never fall, everyone from investors, and workers, to housewives want to join in on this rise… which causes the price to reach completely irrational levels until the first sales occur and the bubble explodes; people panic, everyone wants to sell, the prices start to go down with the same speed as when they went up, sometimes faster, and in those moments many sellers do not have enough buyers so that the price bottoms out, everyone wants to sell and finally, that asset or stock ends up being worthless; this results in many people who bought in or got into debt on the rise going bankrupt, a crisis of confidence begins, the banks stop issuing credit, the economy stops, the panic is set in motion and finally what we know as an economic crisis occurs.

As we shared in chapter three, the two most common causes of crises are brought about by a runaway rise in inflation, and by accelerated debt growth; in both cases the determinant is usually an indiscriminate and unenforced expansion of credit to consumers. This is the model that is most repeated in most financial crises: we saw it in the great depression of 1929 where people borrowed from banks to buy shares from the stock market, we have seen it recently in the crisis of 2008 as well, when banks granted mortgages above the value of a home with additional funds for the purchase of furniture!

In many cases caused by the financial system itself, people settle into a state of euphoria and confidence that triggers consumption and demand for goods of all kinds causing the shares of companies to rise rapidly and therefore the stock market also participates in this joy rising endlessly to dangerous levels. One of the positive things that crises have taught people is to understand that "everything that goes up, must come down". But as the economist John Kenneth Galbraith said in his book "A Brief History of Economic Euphoria" ... "there must be few areas of human activity in which history tells so little as in the field of finance"; in other words, people have a very short memory and forget quickly, which eventually causes a new crisis.

BRIEF HISTORY

We have said that the causes of economic crises are usually different, sometimes they arise from within the economic system itself and sometimes they come from outside and have little to do with the economy, but once these external events arrive they can seriously affect it as we are seeing with the current Covid-19 crisis.

Following, we will make a brief historical review of the main crises and bubbles that have occurred in recent centuries to illustrate what we have been analyzing about the crises.

1637 Tulip crisis in Holand

Although we have already mentioned this crisis caused by the uncontrolled increase in the value of tulip bulbs in Holland, it is a glaring example of human ambition and how far people's irrationality can go every time they encounter a new "el Dorado", whether it is flowers, stocks, or coins or of any other good that rises suddenly and incessantly until the bubble bursts. This fact, caused in a few months the sinking and the subsequent crash of Holland's economy.

1720 Bubble of the South Seas

In England the South Seas Company was created and in France the Banque Royale to absorb and market the public debt of the two States and their companies; they went bankrupt and dragged the whole of Europe into a great recession.

1873 The First Great Recession

There were several causes that came together in the first great recession in 1873: The demonetization of silver in Germany and the United States; speculative investments in the railways, the Franco-Prussian War, and the financial crisis in Vienna in that year caused the crisis to spread throughout Europe.

1929 The Great Depression

It is without a doubt the greatest crisis, the longest and the one that affected the greatest number of countries in the 20th century.

Stock market speculation is at the root of this deep recession that was caused by the large margins and profits that had been obtained in the stock market since 1925 and that after four years of intense speculation stopped in its tracks on Thursday, October 24, 1929, called "Black Thursday"; the collapse of prices was consummated the following Tuesday and the contagion shook the stock markets around the world; the recession made itself felt until after the Second World War.

1973 The Petroleum Crisis

The organization of oil exporting countries (OPEC) turned off the oil tap to all countries that had supported Israel during its war against Syria and Egypt. Suddenly the exporting countries raised the price of oil to quadruple its price; this pushed the world economy into a deep recession that lasted three years.

1997 Asian Financial Crisis

In that year what had been dubbed "the economic miracle of Southeast Asia" crumbled, primarily due to the weakness of their currencies against the dollar; this affected various countries of the region and subsequently all of Asia and the global stock markets. It was the first crisis of the new era of Globalization.

2000 The Dot Com Bubble

The birth of internet startups and the digital sector attracted thousands of investors dazzled by the high returns generated by their shares creating a bubble with very weak foundations, which caused many of these companies not to deliver the expected results. hat spurred the selloff of those shares and the New York stock exchange that was listed in 2000 at more than 5000 points, two years later sank to 1500 points ... more than 5000 Internet (.com) companies went bankrupt.

2008 The Great Recession

Speculation on subprime mortgages by many unscrupulous bankers and betting on the markets turned into real financial casinos caused Lehman Brothers to go bankrupt on September 15 of that year dragging down stock markets around the world... credit was frozen initially between the banks themselves and later to the population with which more than thirty countries began a recession from which to this day, some of them have not fully emerged.

2020 The COVID-19 Depression

We could also call it "The Great Halt" because it has meant that the world has suddenly come to a halt by the invasion of an invisible virus, which has so far caused the biggest recession since the previous one in 1929 without any doubt. It is the most current example we have, which shows that an external phenomenon which is not economic and which has nothing to do with the normal functioning of the economy is capable of affecting it in a more forceful way than by an internal element of the system. However, it is possible to find links with the economy through Globalization as a secondary cause. The consequences and the aftermath that this coronavirus pandemic will leave behind will be felt for many years to come. Let us hope that the application of certified vaccines will limit the spread of the virus to drastically reduce the millions of people affected and the thousands of deaths in the near future and so that we may shorten the recovery time most countries need.

THE CAUSES

In order to be able to see more clearly and to be able to estimate what will be the consequences caused by these phenomena that unleash an economic crisis, we have seen that the effects produced by causes as diverse as the fall of the stock market or a pandemic due to a virus can produce similar damages and harm in the economy.

At first a general alert is generated, soon after the mistrust is imposed between the different economic actors, starting with the banks, then between companies, and finally among the people.

That initial mistrust spreads rapidly to the economic system and suddenly prevents the economy from continuing to function on a regular basis; that is, banks in the face of mistrust stop lending money so that companies that would like to invest and buy machinery to increase their production capacity cannot do so, then the machinery company does not make sales and has to let some workers go, those workers will stop buying food or clothing which means the food or clothing companies will also stop making sales and will also have to let some workers go and the vicious circle expands across the entire economy and finally it becomes an economic recession in every way.

There are other causes that are not strictly economic but rather geopolitical that further exacerbate the duration and depth of crises, such as the recent trade war between the United States and China with the rise in tariffs and the increase in barriers of all kinds that also slow down and impede the normal flow of goods and technology in a globalized economy.

The objective is clear, it is a question of dominance on the world chessboard. On the other hand, the weakness of the dollar due to the large stimuli received by the Federal Reserve together with the strength of the euro are creating distortions in the markets that slow down Europe's exports and make the recovery of the area slower.

Finally, the drop in the price of housing and other assets causes the sense of wealth to decline among citizens; thus, they feel a little poorer and decide to temporarily curb their spending and their demand for durable goods such as cars, housing, leisure, etcetera…

This decrease in general demand, many companies talk about between 50 and 80% fewer sales, produces an over stock in stores, which translates into a drop in prices to try to sell more and finally this causes the profit margins and benefits of many companies to fall and become unsustainable, causing the closure of thousands of them.

THE CONSEQUENCES

The director of the International Monetary Fund, Gina Gopinath, recently said that the impact of the drop in world GDP of 4.5% in 2020 has no precedent in recent economic history, not even in the last financial crisis of 2008 in which the drop was 0.2%. This is the closest thing to a catastrophe and is unprecedented in modern times.

The serious problems being faced by businesses, governments and households are being reflected on a daily basis in the loss of employment, the closure of companies due to a lack of sales and liquidity, the increase in debt at all levels, especially in certain sectors such as airlines, tourism, hospitality, energy, the financial sector, etcetera… although virtually all sectors of the economy are being affected to a greater or lesser extent.

This situation is being supported in some way by the direct and indirect aid measures of the respective governments; but the problem is knowing how long this crisis is going to last or rather this pandemic?… If it is extended for a long time, we run the risk that the munitions that all the States are putting in place will be exhausted, since the level of debt would become unbearable. That is why, as the director of the IMF says, the solution is not going to come from economists or governments, rather it must come, in this case, from healthcare and vaccines to be able to reignite the engines of growth.

Despite the magnitude of this crisis, the most shocking thing is its naturalness and speed. The scenario that is being drawn in almost all the world is a scenario of widespread devastation. Not even very disastrous events in our modern history such as the Civil War and the post-war period or the Great Depression have produced such a steep drop in GDP per capita; in those events as well as in the two world wars, a maximum of 8% was reached. In 2020 the GDP dropped by 12.5% in Spain and by 7% in Europe on average. Each month of confinement means a 1% drop in GDP. Nothing like it has been seen in the last 150 years.

The rapid impoverishment of broad strata of the population had not been seen since the time of the two previous wars, mainly due to the mass layoffs that are taking place; back then, this deterioration took months or years to come, while today in a matter of weeks it has hit everyone, especially the most precarious, temporary and least specialized jobs; although we cannot forget the successive waves of layoffs that we are seeing in other sectors like banks, industry, or in more sophisticated sectors as is happening in some software and telecommunications companies.

In addition to the severe purely economic consequences that companies and other social partners are enduring, it is important to highlight the severity and depth with which this crisis is hitting the most disadvantaged social sectors, such as the unemployed, also, women and children from the lower strata. Once again we are seeing scenes like the ones we have seen in war films with long queues in the soup kitchens or to receive a bag of food; the rise in child poverty has reached 40% in Spain, the increase of homeless people living on the street, or the increase in evictions.

Next, we will analyze and make a historical review of the measures that must be taken primarily on the part of Governments to get out of this situation, as was also done in prior historical periods.

THE EXIT

The two most serious and disastrous events in the previous century were undoubtedly the two world wars. The large number of deaths, the destruction of the productive apparatus of the countries involved and the immense consequences they left on the population are unparalleled in the history of mankind. Both resulted in massive and decisive intervention by governments together with the citizens through reconstruction plans such as the so-called Marshall Plan.

Although the current crisis is not nearly comparable to the disastrous effects left by the two wars, in our opinion, we believe that we are facing the most important challenge facing human rights for decades. It is therefore necessary to implement a new Marshall Plan or for governments to deploy a program of massive aid to the various sectors of society in order to alleviate the serious problems faced by the social partners and the population, which will help them to get out of the current crisis as soon as possible.

In fact, both the European Union and the United States have launched programs in which, in addition to direct aid from governments, the central banks are also participating with monetary easing measures and soft loans, as well as the national banks of each country. However, although this enormous and important support from States is essential from every point of view, also needed at the same time is the cooperation of the civil society. Without community involvement of companies, the self-employed and the citizens' effort, we cannot get out of this situation as soon as possible and it is very likely that the crisis will last for many months longer than desired.

In this sense, in parallel with government aid, it would be necessary to implement other complementary measures such as a more important fiscal effort and control of spending by states and citizens. This is not about looking for the good guys or the bad guys or seeing who is going to foot the bill for this debacle; it is about collaboration among all, in the same way as when a boat is sinking it doesn't help if only a few are rowing, instead the whole crew must row, this will make the boat stay afloat.

However, for that you need a good captain to lead the ship and as the historian Max Hastings said "Western leaders are incredibly incompetent when it comes to explaining tremendously complex situations to the citizenry"; we need leaders with courage and leadership qualities.

Some leaders attribute and hold Globalization responsible for this situation; it is a big mistake, when it is Globalization that has brought the highest levels of well-being and growth in recent decades. Others say we are at war; against whom? where is our enemy? This is a pandemic, a health catastrophe caused by a randomly arrived virus, and what is needed are inspiring leaders as in other periods of history; leaders like a Churchill, or a Roosevelt to act as a reference and that have enough courage to face the harsh reality and give us hope that we will overcome it and that a better future will soon come.

According to a recent study published by Deutsche Bank and signed by its chief strategist, Jim Read, we have reached a new era "The Age of Disorder". "History is made up of cycles, every ten years or so and according to the study, we have reached a supercycle, every 30 or 40 years, which comes after that of Globalization and which is going to bring disorder and uncertainty, protectionism, cold wars, a lot of debt, price volatility, technology everywhere and class and intergenerational struggles; we have been transitioning from one cycle to another for years and Covid-19 has only accelerated this step into a new era of disorder."

Let us hope that, as was the case in the Second World War, a new leader or new leaders such as Churchill will emerge to rescue us from this terrible disaster. The problem is that this type of leader is only born at least once every 100 years. Let us not lose hope.

CONCLUSION

"REINVENTING YOURSELF"

> *"It is crazy to do the same thing over and over again and expect to get different results."*
> *(Albert Einstein)*

We have seen through the various chapters how Globalization, work, the economy, politics, and demography are changing and how these changes are affecting our lives and those of our children today and in the near future. This is not just one more crisis; what we are living with the coronavirus pandemic and with the profound effects and the tremendous negative consequences that it will leave in our lives and in our societies, we can say that what we have had to live is the closest thing to a revolution that will permanently transform our socio-economic model and way of life. It is a paradigm shift where nothing is stable, where only Change will be permanent.

Throughout history there have been other pandemics, other crises and other disasters; however, we do not think they have ever been so global and so frequent. This event is typical of this century, precisely because of the phenomenon of Globalization and the expansion of technology. If anything is differentiating this century from the previous ones in history, it is the multiplication of economic and climate crises, in addition to a distinguishing characteristic, and that is that they happen more and more frequently and also more quickly.

We were not sufficiently prepared for this new scenario of phenomena and events; in fact, the arrival of many of these events has caught most of us, in diapers, as we say colloquially. Therefore the intention of this book is to shed a little light and clarity on what is happening, and also to give some guidelines and some guidance to better understand this great wave that has arrived and that has baffled us all.

Crises and major disasters cause great pain and suffering in the population, although some people and also some countries know how to look at them in a different way, even sometimes more positively, because after the darkness the light usually appears.

History provides us with some examples of relevant men, as we mentioned in the chapter on work, who knew how to re-invent and start a path or a profession totally different from the one they had been performing until then; there are the examples of Blas Pascal who having a promising career as a scientist and because of a serious accident decides to change course and devote himself completely to philosophy. Or the case mentioned above of Emmauel Kant who after practicing law ended up being one of the most important philosophers in the history of thought. Or the novelist, Fyodor Dostoevsky who abandoned a military career to dedicate himself to what he liked best, writing; leaving one of the most representative works of contemporary literature. Or the aforementioned Paul Gauguin who, having worked for years as a stockbroker, changed direction by 180 degrees and became one of the most important impressionist painters of the past century.

Let us look at what China has done; in Chinese, the word crisis has a dual meaning:

"Problem and Opportunity." If we cautiously observe the way in which they have resolved this crisis, which they themselves started, it is truly astounding! On one hand, they have managed to control the pandemic in record time and with a very low death rate, and on the other hand, they have been the first to get on economic recovery train, we only have to look at the growth rates that they are reporting, while in Europe and the United States we are seeing negative growth rates and with very gloomy forecasts for the next two or three years. Does that mean that the Chinese have understood and managed this crisis better, having that word well internalized in their vocabulary, and will they have been able to choose the second meaning? That is, the one that means "Opportunity"... The facts seem to show this up to now.

As in other times throughout history, there have always been people and countries that have been able to take advantage of this kind of event, either through force to conquer other territories, or through new inventions that give them a competitive advantage over others, such as the invention of gunpowder by the Chinese centuries ago, or the invention of the steam engine more recently, or the birth of the Internet in our day.

The detailed observation of history should lead us to reflection on a personal level and as a country, in the sense of taking some time to calmly reflect, analyze and find the strengths and weaknesses that we have, as people and as a country.

It is said that good decisions arise from good thinking and calm. This time we give ourselves for meditation and pause will not be wasted time as it can help us to find perhaps more quickly the best solutions and the most appropriate policies for the time we are living in.

I would like to conclude this book with a message of hope by quoting Stephen Hawking in his book "Brief Responses to the Great Questions" when he says "Intelligence is characterized by the ability to adapt to change. Human intelligence is the result of many generations of natural selection, of those with the ability to adapt to changing circumstances. We should not fear Change. We have to make it work in our favor." Good luck.

THANK YOU!

Thank you for the time you have spent reading "Uncertain Times. The Great Change". If you liked this book and have found it useful I would be very grateful if you leave your opinion on Amazon. It will help me keep writing. Your support is very important. I read all the reviews and try to give feedback to make this book better.

If you wish to contact me, here is my email:

jferrermolina@gmail.com

Thank you for your interest!